OPEN YOUR *Heart* TO *Nature* AND BEYOND

# OPEN YOUR

Heart TO Nature

# AND BEYOND

## DR. LINDA N. CAMERON

# OPEN YOUR HEART TO NATURE AND BEYOND

*iUniverse books may be ordered through booksellers or by contacting:*

*iUniverse*
*1663 Liberty Drive*
*Bloomington, IN 47403*
*www.iuniverse.com*
*844-349-9409*

*ISBN: 978-1-6632-2366-1 (sc)*
*ISBN: 978-1-6632-2369-2 (e)*

*Library of Congress Control Number: 2021910588*

*Print information available on the last page.*

*iUniverse rev. date: 09/09/2021*

# Contents

# Acknowledgements

In writing this book, I stand on the shoulders of giants not only in the world of religion but in poetry, philosophy, psychology, and physics — and to various individuals in each of these disciplines, I am very grateful and honor the ideas and wisdom present in their works of knowledge. I would also like to thank individuals in my personal life particularly those in my weekly spiritual groups whose questions challenged me to refine my thinking about some of the ideas presented in this book. So here is a salute of gratitude to Rosalee Kinast, Pat and Martina Griffing, and Lexa Gurmendi. I would particularly like to thank Beloved Jesus and Mary not only for their emotional support during my life but for directing me to the writings of others to amplify and augment an understanding of my religious experiences of the Divine.

# Chapter 1

## THE PURE IN HEART

**Blessed are the pure in heart; for they shall see God.**
**Matthew 5:8**

In the Sermon on the Mount, Jesus stated that "the pure in heart will see God" (Matthew 5:8). I concluded from this scripture that being "pure in heart" meant that we had to be perfect in order to have an experience of the Divine or I AM Presence while here in the physical world. I did believe it was possible to be perfect because traditional Christian scriptures teach that we were created in the image of God; and thus, we have perfection within us. Genesis 1:27 states "So God created man in his own image, in the image of God created he him; male and female he created them." Psalm 82: 6 states "I have said, Ye are gods; and all of you are children of the Most High." Jesus affirms this scripture from the Old Testament in John 10:34 saying "Is it not written in your law, I said, Ye are gods?" Some individuals believe "Ye are gods" refers to the fact that some humans represent God as messengers but the word used in this passage is "theos" which is the Greek word for God and not "angeliaforos which is the Greek word for messenger."

Beloved Jesus again affirms that the kingdom is within us in Luke 17:20-21 when he states, "...The kingdom of God cometh not with observation. Neither shall they say, Lo Here! Or, lo there! For, behold, the kingdom of God is in the midst of you." Stephen Mitchell in *The Gospel According to Jesus* maintains that the King James version of the

Bible incorrectly translated Luke 17:20-21 where Jesus says, "Behold the Kingdom of God is in the midst of you." He points out the King James Version erroneously interprets the Greek preposition *entos* to mean "among" or "in the middle of" when, in fact it means "within" and this difference changes the entire meaning of the verse.

In the *Hebrew-Greek Keyword Study Bible KJV* edited by Spiros Zodhiates, Th. D. and Warren Baker, D.R.E. the word "within" is used in the Luke 17:21 passage instead of "in the midst of" and thus reads as "Neither shall they say, Lo here! Or, lo there! For, behold, the kingdom of God is within you." The meaning of this single word determines whether our spiritual path to an experience of the Divine primarily involves a walk inward within ourselves or outward into the world. In the Gospel of Mary from the *Nag Hammadi" Library of the Great Gnostic Writings*, Jesus reportedly said, "Beware that no one lead you astray, Say Lo here! Lo there! For the Son of Man is within you. Follow after him!" In the Gospel of Saint Thomas from the *Dead Sea Scrolls* Jesus is reported to say:

If those who lead you say to you; see, the kingdom is in Heaven,

then the birds of heaven will proceed you.

If they say to you: It is in the sea, then the fish will precede you.

But the Kingdom is within you and it is without you.

If you know yourselves, then you will be known and you will

Know that you are the sons of the Living Father.

But if you do not know yourselves, then you are in poverty

And you are poverty.

Not only are we created in the image of God; we have been given the ability to use the power of God to control nature and perform miracles in the world. Is there anything in the Bible stating that we have such power over nature? Yes, we are told in the Old Testament that we have "Dominion over the fish of the sea, and over the fowl of the air, and over the cattle, and over all the earth, and over every creeping thing that creepeth upon the earth" (Genesis 1:26). The Hebrew word for dominion is *"radah"* which refers to rule over or subjugate. The word dominion is defined in *The Random House Dictionary of the English Language* as "sovereign authority or the power or right of governing and controlling". Traditionally, the idea of dominion has been interpreted to justify humankind's right to use nature to meet its own ends. Nature's resources are plundered to build houses, supply food, and provide transportation without any sense of appreciation, honor, or respect for the services rendered by these kingdoms of God.

Although many believe that we have been given dominion over the mineral, plant, and animal kingdoms, few people understand that this dominion actually involves commanding nature to do things. Many of us have been taught the scientific view of the world of nature as being powerful, and we are mere puppets or pawns enveloped by this mighty force when the exact opposite is true. For example, we are told in 1 John 4:4, "Ye are of god, little children … greater is he that is in you, than he that is in the world." And in 1 John 5:4 we are also told, "For whatsoever is born of God overcometh the world…"

Throughout the New Testament, we can see how nature can be controlled and changed by a mere command of spoken words from Jesus. In Luke 8:24 and Matthew 8:26, Jesus rebuked the wind and water. Immediately, they obeyed ceasing their activity and there was calm. In Luke 9:16, it is reported that Jesus precipitated the number of fishes from two and the amount of the bread from five loaves to feed the multitude gathered to hear His Sermon on the Mount. Moreover, in Matthew 21:21-22, Jesus is reported to have ordered the death of a fig tree and it "withered away."

Traditional Christians generally believe that only Jesus can do these types of miracles and we must go through Him to accomplish such feats. However, in John 1:12, it is written, "But as many as received him, to them gave He power to become the children of God, even to them that believe on His name." Again, in John 14:12, Jesus asserts, "Verily, verily, I say unto you, he that believeth on me, the works that I do shall he do also; and greater works than these shall he do; because I go unto my Father." Jesus also told the people when He healed them physically that it was their faith that healed them (Mark 5:34, Mark 10:52; Luke 8:48, and Luke 17:19).

The idea that we lack the ability to control nature and heal others also contradicts Old Testament reports that Moses, Elijah, and Elisha performed similar miracles and healings through their connection with God. Moses showed how a man can be instrumental in controlling nature. He performed amazing miracles while leading the Jewish people out of Egypt and into the Promised Land. In Exodus 17:4-6, Moses smote the rock with his rod and water came out so the people could drink. In Exodus 14:21 Moses "Stretched out his hand over the sea; and the Lord caused the sea to go back by a strong wind all that night, and made the sea dry land, and the waters were divided." Like Moses, Elijah and Elisha, great prophets in Old Testament times were also reported to have controlled water. Elijah (2 Kings 2: 8) and Elisha (2 Kings 2:12-14) both smote the waters, which separated and allowed the prophets to cross to the other side on dry ground.

Elijah also brought a woman's son back to life in 1 Kings 17:17-24 and was instrumental in both stopping the rain and in bringing the rain (1 Kings 18: 41-46). In the New Testament, Elijah's ability to affect the rain is referred to in James 5: 17-18. Elijah is considered to be "A man subject to like passions as we are, and he "prayed earnestly that it might not rain; and it rained not on the earth by the space of three years and six months" and he "prayed again, and the earth brought forth her fruit."

Although I believed that I was created in God's image, I also knew that I was unable to consistently manifest this perfection in my daily life as commanded by Jesus during the Sermon on the Mount. Jesus said "Be ye perfect as your Father in Heaven is perfect (Matthew 5:48). At the same time, I knew I was unable to perform miracles or have nature obey my commands. As a result, during my teenage years, I gave up my spiritual search for an experience of the Divine, as well as attempts to precipitate changes in nature. I believed such requests were unattainable for me. So I turned outward to the physical world to fill my empty heart. I did find momentary excitement and pleasure, but they did not last. During my college years in undergraduate school, I became an agnostic and doubted the reality of God after encountering Darwin's Theory of Evolution in a biology course in college. I remember thinking at this time that God was just another Santa Claus myth. But I should point out that I did not give up prayers of supplication whenever I got myself into a mess while roaming in the wilderness of life.

During the final years of my training to be a psychologist, I returned to my spiritual quest following a rather powerful and fearful experience while driving around the shoreline of a lake in Waco, Texas. I was listening to music in my car when suddenly the question "What is all of this?" came into my mind. It was very frightening to me because I could not answer this question. I knew about the Big Bang Theory and Darwinian Theory of Evolution but for me, these answers did not satisfactorily answer the question, "What is all of this?" Instead, every time this question came into my mind, fear would radiate throughout my body. Panic would set in at this time. Fortunately, a few weeks later I had a dream that stopped the panic and answered this question to my satisfaction.

The dream involved just one scene. The background of this dream was totally dark and in foreground was a single, white, burning candle. As I watched this burning candle with my dream eye, a voice said: "From Whom all Blessings Flow." I woke up startled and remembered this was from the doxology, "Praise God from whom all blessings flow." We sang this on Sunday mornings during my childhood years at Saint Mary's Episcopal Church in Kinston, North Carolina when the offering was dedicated at the altar. I then said out loud to myself, "Oh my God there is a God! Although I was still unable to maintain perfection on a daily basis, I dedicated myself to learning how to become pure in heart. I joined Saint Paul's Episcopal church in Waco, Texas where I was living at the time and began reading Pierre Teilhard de Chardin's *The Phenomenon of Man* a book which attempted to integrate science and Christianity and hypothesized that Jesus introduced the concept of a phylum of love into evolutionary theory. I remember thinking at the time that the scientific study of evolutionary theory in biology took me away from God and now through the works of de Chardin, a Jesuit priest in the Catholic church, it was bringing me back to God.

My studies of biblical history revealed that such biblical heroes as Moses, David, and Saint Paul were also imperfect in their behaviors even committing murders. Yet, they had very powerful encounters with God and brought forth mighty revelations of the Divine. It is interesting to note that most of the Bible is written by murderers. Moses is credited with writing the first 5 books of the Bible including Genesis, Exodus, Leviticus, Numbers, and Deuteronomy. David wrote 72 of the Psalms and Saint Paul wrote Romans, 1 and 2 Corinthians, Galatians, Ephesians, Colossians, 1 and 2 Thessalonians, 1 and 2 Timothy, Titus, and Philemon.

After murdering an abusive Egyptian, Moses fled Egypt and settled in the Land of Midian. While tending his father-in-law's flock of sheep, Moses spotted a blazing fire in the middle of a bush on Mount Sinai. Amazed that the bush engulfed in flames did not disintegrate, he went to investigate and God then called, "Moses! Moses!" "Here I am!" Moses replied (Exodus 3:4). Then the Lord God told Moses that he was to lead people out of Egypt (Exodus 3:7-13). Moses then asked God what name should he use to tell the people who sent him. And God replied to Moses, "I Am that I Am" (Exodus 3:14).

King David, also in the Old Testament, was selected by God Himself who considered him to be a man after His own heart. In Samuel 16:7, God told Samuel that "He had rejected Saul as King of Israel" and to go to Bethlehem as He had selected one of the sons of Jesse to be the new King of Israel. When Jesse's youngest son David was called from the field ...the Lord said, "This is the one" (Samuel 16: 12). However, as time progressed, King David became not only an adulterer but a murderer. In 2 Samuel 11: 4-5, David is reported to have committed adultery when he lay with Bath-Sheba and she conceived, and told David she was with child. David then devised a scheme to murder Bathsheba's husband Uriah. In 2 Samuel 11:15 David sent a letter to Joab saying "...Set ye Uriah in the forefront of the hottest battle, and retire ye from him, that he may be smitten, and die." Paul is another example of a murderer having a profound experience of the Divine or I AM Presence. In I Corinthians 15:9, Paul says he "persecuted the church of God" and in Acts 22:4, he persecuted "unto death, binding

6

and delivering into prisons both men and women." All of this came to a stop following an experience on the road to Damascus when "Suddenly there shined round about him a light from heaven" (Acts 9:3). He fell to the ground and heard a voice saying to him Saul! Saul! Why are you persecuting me?" (Acts 9:4). He was then told that he had been chosen to be a witness of God to men.

Having accepted that Moses, David, Saint Paul, Elijah, and Elisha all had powerful experiences of the Divine and Moses, Elijah, Elisha, and Saint Paul were also able to control nature and perform miracle healings despite great flaws in their behavior, I decided that I must have misinterpreted the verse "only the pure in heart will see God" (Mathew 5:8). It does not mean we have to be perfect to have an encounter with the Divine or to perform healings and command nature. But what then is required to have such experiences?

Clues pointing to an answer to this question can be found in I Samuel 13:14 where God said that He "hath sought him a man (David) after his own heart." In I Samuel 16:7, "The Lord said unto Samuel, "Look not on his countenance, or on the height of his statue, because I have refused him; for the Lord seeth not as man seeth; for man looketh on the outward appearance, but the Lord looketh on the heart." It seems clear from these statements that God considers the heart of a person to be of prime importance and not necessarily outward appearances and behaviors.

During earlier times the heart was considered to be of great importance in many religions around the world. In *Resilience from the Heart: The Power to Thrive in Life's Extremes*, Gregg Braden points out that the *Egyptian Book of the Dead* describes a ceremony performed at one's death called the "Weighing of the Heart." The dead person's heart was literally weighed to determine if he or she could proceed into the afterlife.

References to the heart in Christianity appear in all but seven books of the Bible suggesting that it held an important place within these religious teachings as well. In the Catholic Church, there are images of Jesus and Mary opening their clothing to show their Sacred Hearts. Moreover, there is an annual celebration of the Feast of the Sacred

Heart. The symbol of the Sacred Heart evolved from the mystical experiences and visions of many Roman Catholic nuns, including Saint Lutgarde, Saint Mechtilde, Saint Gertrude, and Saint Margaret Mary Alocoque. Following multiple apparitions between the years of 1673 and 1675 in which Jesus appeared to Saint Margaret Mary Alacoque and revealed his great love and sympathy of mankind, she accepted His call for her to devote her life to loving and caring for others. In her forth vision, Jesus instructed her that a Feast of the Scared Heart should be celebrated each year. Eventually, in 1856, Pope Pius IX decreed the annual celebration of the Feast of the Sacred Heart in the Catholic Church on June 8th of each year.

With the passage of time, most people came to believe that scriptural references to listen, know, and act with the heart were merely metaphors for being a loving person. This can be seen in the idea of the Sacred Heart in the Catholic Church. Within these teachings, the heart is considered to be the center of being, both physical and spiritual. It represents compassion, understanding, love, and charity. It also represents the temple of God, His divine center and dwelling place. The pierced and bleeding heart alludes to the manner of Jesus' death and reveals to us Christ's goodness and charity through His wounds and ultimate sacrifice. When our love and compassion triumphs over our egos, our spirits will be liberated, and they will transform our entire beings into a holy ones. If we align ourselves with meaning of the Sacred Heart and the liberating vibration of Christ consciousness, this great symbol can become a gateway for us to change the world through our expression of unequivocal, genuine love.

The belief that the heart involved mostly being a loving person began to change with the "I AM" teachings that started with Helen Petrovna Blavatsky (8/12/1831 – 5/8/1891) in her first published book *Isis Unveiled* and who formed the Theosophy Society, as well as Alice Anne Bailey (6/16/1880 – 12/15/1949) who developed the Arcane School and authored the "blue books" which contain teachings similar to the Theosophy Society of Blavatsky but did differ in many respects.

Again, in the 1930's, the "I AM" teachings of Mr. G. W. Ballard (7/28/1878 – 12/29/1939) and later his wife Edna Ballard

(6/25/1886 – 2/10/1971) came forth in the "green books" and emphasized the importance of the heart and freedom. These "I AM" teachings maintain that when we open our hearts, we are connecting with the mind of God or the "I AM" Presence and the real function of our minds is to channel this wisdom and love from the heart into our world.

Following the death of Mr. Ballard, Geraldine Innocenti, who died June 21, 1961, left the Saint Germain "I AM" Institute in Chicago, Illinois and formed the Bridge to Freedom "I AM" teachings in Philadelphia and dictated what ultimately became the "white books" which repeated some of the teachings of the Saint Germain "I AM" dictations by Mr. G.W. Ballard but added new ones that came through her. *The Twelve Powers of Man* written during the 1930's by Charles Filmore, founder of Unity Church, states that "Man receives first an intellectual understanding of Truth which he translates to the heart, where love is awakened…and head knowledge must decrease as heart understanding increases." In *The Intelligent Heart*, authors Davis McArthur and Bruce McArthur state that "Head knowledge switches its role and becomes a facilitator for the heart wisdom —the head's role shifts from being the commander-in-chief of the system to being an effective general under the heart's leadership."

In *The Hidden Power of the Heart*, Sara Patterson states that the "head is to sort, process, assess, calculate, memorize, and compare," while the "heart gives a broader perspective from which to view head information." She discusses a vision that she had regarding what she calls a "heart crystal pattern." She reported seeing in the heart "infinite crystals in a cornucopia shape and realized each crystal had a different intelligent frequency band." These crystals contained a person's present, past, and future records in a holographic formation of crystal-like chips in the heart.

Not only has wisdom been associated with the heart, but the emotion of love has again been emphasized as a way to open the heart to receive wisdom. In Christian religious teachings, Jesus spells out what emotion we should have toward the Divine in our hearts. He calls us to "Love the Lord, thy God, with all thy heart, and with all thy soul, and with all thy mind in Matthew 22:37." Psalm 50:14 states that we must

"Offer unto God thanksgiving" as thanksgiving and gratitude are keys to a loving heart. These scriptures of having an open and loving heart to experience the Divine dovetail with the scientific findings from the Institute of HeartMath, a pioneering research organization founded by Mr. D. L. Childre in the 1990s to study the full potential of the human heart. Their basic technique to gain a coherent heart begins with visioning and feeling a spirit of thanksgiving, appreciation, or gratitude within oneself just as was suggested in Psalm 50:14. Doing this leads to a feeling of being a loving spirit as Jesus commanded us to do in Matthew 22:37 and this produces a coherent heart and its rewards of a reduced cortisol stress hormone level, lower heart rate, and other autonomic nervous system activities that mediate the fight/flight stress response in the body.

Most of us do not have a coherent heart; rather, we have what the Bible calls *hardened hearts* and this not only prevents encounters with the Divine but blocks our ability to heal and control nature spiritually. The next chapter will explore the nature of our harden hearts so that we can return to a pure heart and thereby experience the Divine and reclaim the powers to command nature as we were authorized to do at creation.

# Chapter 2

## THE HARDENED HEART

**And the Lord said unto Moses, Pharaoh's heart is
hardened, he refuseth to let the people go.
Exodus 7: 14**

What a price the Pharaoh of Egypt paid by having a hardened heart. His closed heart caused the people of his country to suffer many plagues, pestilences, livestock deaths, hail, fire, and personally, the loss of his own son. We are warned about having a hardened or closed heart in many places in the Bible. In Hebrews 3:8, we are told, "Harden not your hearts" and in Matthew 13:15 Jesus warns that a hardened heart prevents us from seeing God and hearing His truth. With a hardened heart, we do not see the truth; rather, "we see in a mirror, darkly" (I Corinthians 13:12). This refers to the idea that we project our hardened heart onto people, events, and things outside of ourselves and then see our own dark heart mirrored back to us, which we mistakenly believe is some external truth. Psychology calls this process projection and, in Matthew 7: 5, Jesus evidences an awareness of this process in His call for us to "First cast the beam out of thine own eye; and then shalt thou see clearly to cast out the mote out of thy brother's eye."

What is a hardened heart? A harden heart results when we form and hold onto external relationships with people, events, and things to fill the void we create within ourselves when we walk away from God. These relationships create a merry-go-round of holding onto and separation from the Divine that whirls us about throughout our lifetimes. Buddha considered such attachments to be the root of all suffering and thought they blocked experiences of Nirvana, the state beyond all desires for attachment. Carl McColman in *The Aspiring Mystic* believes that the three most powerful attachments are to money, sex, and power. He explains this is why monasteries require vows of poverty, chastity, and obedience. He also points out that even our efforts of self-discipline and endurance can also easily become attachments.

*A Course in Miracles* calls these alliances with the external world "special" relationships, which emphasizes the qualities of attraction, importance, and exaltation that characterize the way we feel in them. But I prefer to use the term "holding" to characterize them because it better defines the way they prevent us from uniting with the Divine. Holding onto false ideas about ourselves and our relationships to things, people, events, and actions in the world is the antithesis of letting go in order to connect and flow with the Divine in the Great River of Life.

Our holding relationships can take many forms, but their purpose is always the same: attempts to bolster, maintain, or hide our false self-images and the inner states of inflation or deflation that accompanies them. Such relationships do provide temporary feelings of pleasure and fleeting, illusory experiences of wholeness, which compel us to continually seek and cling to them. However, they also diminish awareness of the Divine within us, thereby preventing us from joining with the "breath of life."

Now, let's look at the various holding relationships we use to cope with our false self-images and their inner states of inflation and deflation. The first holding relationship we form in life is with ourselves. This determines the nature of our other holding relationships. In our psychological development, rather than accept the image of God within us and believe we are good, we separate from the Divine within. Hence, we are also isolated from its many positive emotional fruits—love, joy, peace, longsuffering, faith gentleness, goodness, meekness, and temperance (Galatians 5:22-23).

Although our free will enables us to push the Divine and its fruits away, we can't eliminate them from our beings. Like the setting sun, they remain below the horizon waiting for us to welcome them back into awareness. Rejection of the Divine and its fruits do, however, create a vacuum in our beings, and just as darkness follows a sunset, a sense of lacking, aloneness, and helplessness arises within us when we distance ourselves from the image of God within us. The type of darkness we experience is determined by which aspect of our divine nature we reject. For example, if we push our inner love out of our awareness, we will feel fear. If we lose awareness of our inner power, then we will feel weak and helpless.

The uncomfortable, dark place that we create when we reject awareness of the Divine within compels us to do something for relief, so we construct masks in which we redefine ourselves in our own terms. Although our new self-image may include some parts of the Divine and its fruits, it excludes others, and is less than whole. Therefore, it is a false image of ourselves. This false image not only still leave us feeling empty, lacking, and helpless at times, they also create inner states of inflation and deflation. So why do we keep the Divine within us outside of our awareness? We do so because it is better to avoid the Divine within than to face a God we secretly fear will punish us for separating from Him.

If we judge our holding relationships with ourselves as negative, we can fall into a fixed state of deflation and feel depressed most of the time. Here, we believe our negative false identity to be real, and we condemn it as unworthy. We then worship our own unworthiness by constantly chanting to ourselves a litany of reasons why we are lacking, guilty, bad, unlovable, powerless, or unworthy. Although the reasons that we give for our unworthiness are many and varied, they are all equally invalid.

Many religions teach that we harbor the Divine within us; therefore, humankind is basically good. Hinduism speaks of Atman or the Eternal within that lies behind our mass of distractions and ego assumptions. The Navajos believe that first Man and First Woman were born from ears of corn when the wind blew the breath of life into an ear of white corn and yellow corn, respectively. Islam believes that man has forgotten his divinity and is fundamentally good. Within the Christian tradition we are told in Genesis 1:27-31 that "God created man in His own image. . ... blessed them . . . And God saw that everything that He had made . . . was very good." Now, true humility would be to agree with God's assessment of us as being "very good." But instead, we create false images of ourselves as being unworthy, lacking, alone, powerless, and unlovable and then castigate ourselves for these qualities. This seems arrogant to me for two reasons. First, maintaining that we are not what God says we are indirectly involves telling God that He is wrong. Either God is telling us the truth about ourselves, which we believe is false, or what we believe is true and what God is saying is false. We can't have it both ways. Secondly, it presumes that we are more powerful than God because we believe that we can change what He wills to be. Namely, it entails the belief that we can make ourselves into something that is entirely different from what God created us to be.

Although we cherish our false beliefs about ourselves, we are at the same time unhappy with them. All my life, I have heard people speak negatively about themselves, but to this day, I have yet to hear anyone say, "I'm horrible and I love it." In most cases we dislike the terrible person that we conjure up and see in the mirror. I think this suggests that our negative self-conceptions are false. For example, if I am a murderer in my heart and murder someone, I will be perfectly content and there will be no dissonance in my mind. However, if I'm not a murderer in my heart and murder someone, I will be unhappy and discontented within myself. The same seems true to me regarding my self-view. If I'm created good, as Genesis says I am, but view myself as bad, then I will experience dissonance between my feelings and my thoughts.

Although we could easily let go of our negative self-images, many of us choose instead to layer over them with a holier-than-thou attitude. This is generally known by the name of pride. Here we repress or hide our negative beliefs about ourselves from conscious awareness and then project them onto others. We now see ourselves as vastly superior to other people, whom we see as lacking, guilty, bad, inferior, or having some other negative characteristic. This is why people typically dislike a proud person. Without ever speaking a word, a proud person tells us through his or her negative projections onto us that we are inferior and lacking.

Debbie Ford in *Dark Side of the Light Chasers* defines this process of repression and condemnation but maintains that we need to own and embrace both our negative and positive attributes in order to achieve wholeness. Like psychiatrist Carl Jung, she believes that "to be divine is to be whole and to be whole is to be everything: the positive and the negative, the good and the bad, the holy man and the devil." I agree that we need to shine the light of consciousness on both our positive and negative characteristics and then accept, not condemn them. I also believe that we need to let go of the negative qualities, which come from our false self-images in order to unite with the Divine and regain awareness of the positive attributes of our divine nature and thereby experience our wholeness. Can we really experience our wholeness by accepting our lack or by letting our sense of lack go with the Law of Forgiveness?

We can also form inflated, rather than deflated holding relationships with ourselves. Such narcissism results from an unconscious identification with the Divine within. We usurp the throne of the Divine within us, crown ourselves as gods, and believe that we are the center of the universe around which others should revolve. We believe ourselves to be above the rules and regulations that others abide by. I remember encountering such a narcissistic person at the local lake where I did sunset medications. The way he behaved showed that he felt he was above the rules of shared living. The first indication of his narcissism could be seen in the way that he parked his SUV diagonally across three longitudinally lined parking spaces. Secondly, he was at the lake swimming and wind surfing in defiance of the sign at the entrance to the park that clearly stated "No Swimming." Finally, in violation of local leash laws he was letting his two dogs run around loose when I entered the park. On three prior occasions, my dog Monty had been attacked and bitten by several dogs allowed to run loose in the park. So, to prevent any problems, I left Monty in the car, walked toward this guy, and called to him to secure his dogs. I spoke firmly but politely and said, "Would you please leash your dogs." His response was to yell an obscenity at me. Narcissistic people typically display such anger at being corrected because they interpret it as an attack on their perfectionism from a clearly inferior person.

Not wanting any trouble, I returned to my car and feeling tired of people being irresponsible with their dogs, I decided to call the police. While waiting for them arrive, I realized that I needed to work through my own anger if I was to have good meditation that day. After letting my anger go, I noticed the guy approaching my car with a dominating stare on his face while his dogs circled around. I simply ignored him and tried to quite my now barking dog. He left the vicinity of my car and for 15-20, minutes he played with his unleashed dogs. He again returned to the front of my car and stood there staring. I continued to avoid his attempt to engage me in a fight. He finally left, walked over to his SUV, and leashed his dogs. My intuition told me that he figured the police would soon arrive. Sure enough, when the police came, he had his dogs on a leash. I overheard him lying to the police about what had happened. He told the policeman that he put the dogs on leashes when requested and that I simply chose to sit in the car. Lying to maintain the illusion of perfection is very characteristic of the narcissistic personality. At this point, I could only smile at what he was saying. Yes, I thought to myself, I would much rather call the police and sit in my car here at the lake than to join the Divine in a sunset meditation.

The type of holding relationship that we have with ourselves also determines the type of emotions that we experience. Many professionals believe that emotions such as anxiety, anger, and depression are merely biochemical changes in the brain and physical reactions in the body in response stimuli in the outside world. Therefore, traditional medicine treats these feelings by changing the biochemical properties of the brain with such drugs as Valium, Zoloft, Paxil, and Prozac.

Psychologically, these emotions with their bodily changes are typically interpreted as resulting from our interactions with the outside world. But this view slights the importance of thought in producing our emotions. I believe that thinking precedes an emotion, which is a mere translation of, say, anxious, angry, or depressive thoughts from the mind into the body via the autonomic nervous system. The thoughts that produce feelings in the body are as unconscious as those associated with riding a bicycle or driving a car, but they are there never the less. In *The Little Book of Letting Go*, Hugh Prather also maintains emotions are by-products of thinking.

Although people and situations in the world are not the cause of our emotions, they can reveal the thoughts that produce them and are in need of correction. For example, if our holding relationship with ourselves is one that doubts some aspect of our divine nature such as our love, power, or worthiness, then we feel anxious and typically begin an outer search to restore it in some holding relationship. Such doubts also leave us sensitized to perceiving people and situations as the source of our fears. We all have areas of sensitivity in our personalities that give us certain tendencies in interpreting the world around us. For example, if we doubt the existence of our inner love, then we tend to interpret most external events as taking love from us. Thus, we respond with increased fear to these people and situations. The type of fear that we experience and are sensitized to depends upon which aspect of our divine nature we originally doubted. By examining our interpretations of the people and situations that we fear, we can identify and correct the thoughts that elicit them.

Now if we have thoughts that attack rather than doubt attributes of our Divine nature, we will feel hurt and lacking in these fruits. Consequently, anger then layers over our hurts as a defense against further hurt. Just like we do with anxiety, we look without to restore the attributes that we have attacked within ourselves by forming holding relationships. We also become sensitized to interpret our surroundings as attacking us, and consequently we increase our hurt and anger even more. The type of hurt and anger that we experience is directly related to the attribute or attributes of our divine nature that we have attacked and distanced from our awareness. Again, by examining our interpretations of the people and situations that we believe hurt and angered us, we can identify and correct the thoughts that aroused them.

If at this point, we turn our anger inward and beat ourselves with our own angry thoughts, we experience depression. And as we did in our search to end anxiety, we look to our holding relationships to deal with it. We are also sensitized to interpreting external events as depressing us rather than seeing our own thinking as producing this feeling. Examining our interpretations of depressing events have the potential of revealing the thoughts that cause them and need to be undone. Again, the type of depression that we experience is determined by the attribute or attributes of our divine nature that we originally attacked, distanced ourselves from, and then felt hurt and anger about.

Believing that people and events in the world cause us to feel anxiety, anger, and depression results in our feeling vulnerable; we feel like puppets pulled by the strings of the external world. It is only by becoming aware of the destructive thoughts that produce these emotional upsets and letting them go that we can reconnect with the Divine within us and feel whole again. By uniting with the Divine, we can experience the fruits of our divine nature and feel whole again as our love, power, goodness, control, patience, gentleness, faith, and sense of worthiness quietly returns to us.

The type of holding relationship that we have with ourselves also determines the type we form with our bodies. Here, we seek to restore the Divine nature that we rejected when we created our false identities through attachments to our body. Instead of identifying with the Divine within, we consider ourselves to be only bodies and then form positive, negative, or both positive and negative holding relationships with them. We form these types of holding relationships by making our self-esteem, our sense of power, and our lovability based upon such physical attributes as our looks, our weight, or our muscle power. If our physical attributes meet or exceed the acceptable cultural norm, then we feel worthy, powerful, and loveable. In this case, our holding relationship with our bodies is positive but only in the sense that we gain positive feelings about ourselves from the physical attributes of our body. But such feelings based on our body of course doom us to instability because they are fleeting and illusory. Moreover, they can encourage us to use our bodies to feed our egos' inflation so we end seeing ourselves as better than others. On the other hand, if our body deviates from the norm negatively, our sense of worthiness, power, and lovability can diminish until we become deflated and feel inferior to other people. In this case, our holding relationship with our body is negative in that it produces negative feelings about ourselves. Most people have negative holding relationships with at least some part of their body: a nose that is too long or too wide, feet that are too big or too small, hands that are too fat or too thin, and so on. A negative holding relationship with the body is as fleeting and illusory as a positive one, but differs in that it generates and perpetuates alienation or ego deflation that causes us to see others as better than ourselves.

Whether the relationship that we have with our body is positive or negative is less important than the fact that we try to use it to restore the attributes of our divine nature. This sets us up for a bipolar roller coaster ride with the external world. When we base such attributes as joy, worthiness, power, and lovability on the body, we are forming and holding onto relationships that cause up and down cycling in our lives. If we see others with bodies better than ours, we feel down and deflated. Conversely, when we see others with bodies worse than ours, we feel up or inflated.

These holding relationships with the body also block our connection to the Divine within us. Only when we become aware of these holding relationships and let them go can we unite with the Divine. When we connect with the Divine within us, we anchor our self-esteem into something that is unchangeable and that provides a still point from which to view a turning world. Now, we can feel the true attributes of our divine nature and end our bipolar puppet dance with the world. Instead of holding onto our bodies to restore our divine nature and deal with our inflation and deflation, we can let go and flow with the Divine within us.

We can also use our bodies as reservoirs of repressed conflicts and physical manifestations of our states of inflation and deflation, which ultimately leads to disorder in our bodies. The work of Cannon and Hans Selye helped me understand this category of holding relationships with the body. They pointed out the importance of the autonomic nervous system in producing changes that are associated with our physical reactions to stress. I could now see that the thoughts and conflicts associated with our states of inflation and deflation trigger the autonomic nervous system to produce physical changes in the form of stress reactions in the body. Across time, these stress reactions in the body result in disease and disorder.

Just as we have holding relationships with ourselves and our bodies, we can have them with other people. These, too, are attempts to fill the vacuum resulting from our separation for the Divine within us. *In Forgiveness and Jesus*, Dr. Kenneth Wapnick details how *A Course in Miracles* views such holding relationships. All relationships, he says, begin with special love between two people, each of whom uses the other's love to mask over his or her own negative feelings and deficiencies. Neither really loves the other for himself or herself but rather for what he or she can give. When such special love is not forthcoming, the special love relationship can quickly turn into a special hate relationship. This is why two lovers can very quickly turn into two haters.

Rejecting the attributes of our Divine nature creates an inner void that we try to restore by getting them from others. We come to our relationships with others believing that our cup is empty, and they must fill it so that we can feel whole and happy. We form holding relationships with other people and settle for the crumbs of love, power, or worthiness that they toss to us. We then use these crumbs to replace our rejected attributes, patch over negative feelings, and silence the thoughts of our false identities. Such holding relationships actually increase our dependency upon others, whom we now need desperately in order to keep our sense of wholeness and happiness alive.

Like our holding relationships with ourselves and with our bodies, the holding relationships with other people also set us up for a bipolar ride. When other people give us the love, power, and sense of worthiness that we have rejected within ourselves, we feel whole and happy again. If they are displeased with us and fail to deliver what we want from them, then we crash into unhappiness and alienation. However, if we maintain our connection with the Divine and thereby the attributes of our divine nature, we come to our relationships with a full cup and can actually love others for themselves instead of for ourselves. We can love people more because we need them less. We can accept and love them regardless of their behavior toward us because we do not need them to behave in a certain way to maintain our own wholeness and happiness. We are no longer puppets dancing to the pull of other people. We have stopped our roller coaster ride with them and instead have found our inner still point with the Divine.

Like our holding relationships with ourselves and our bodies, our holding relationships with others can be transformed into holy relationships. How? By approaching them as classrooms in which we learn of our disconnection from the Divine and its fruits. By observing what we seek in others, we can become conscious of what we have rejected in ourselves. If we are constantly looking for love from other people, we are obviosity not aware that it is already inside of us. If we seek for power, control, or respect from others, then clearly, we don't know that we are already in possession of these qualities. After identifying what we look for in our holding relationships with others, we can then let go of our outer search for these qualities. Thus, we can reconnect to the Divine within, and thereby to such divine qualities as joy, peace, love, power, and goodness. In this way, our holding relationships with others can be used to reunite with the Divine, and to establish holy relationships with those around us.

Another broad area of holding relationships that we form centers around the external world of things. These also reflect the type of holding relationships that we have with ourselves. We form holding relationships with things in the world in order to fill up the sense of emptiness that comes when we push the Divine and its attributes out of our awareness. We tend to form relationships with things as either Incorporators or Achievers. Incorporators try to undo inner emptiness and its negative states by incorporating material things from the external world into their bodies or into their lives. They incorporate, take in, or cannibalize the world in an attempt to recapture their wholeness. Incorporators can be food users or drug abusers because they take these substances into their bodies to cover feelings, sedate pain, or restore wholeness.

Other people in this group incorporate things into their life space. They focus on gaining and possessing material things to obtain wholeness and restore the lost attributes of their divine nature. Achievers, on the other hand, try to regain wholeness through action. They appear in many forms and in many places. Sports competitors, workaholics, and thrill seekers are all trying to achieve wholeness and change states of inflation and deflation by challenging, manipulating, and controlling the external world. But these efforts are at best fleeting and illusory. They are doomed because wholeness and its attributes come only by reconnecting with the Divine. It awaits our welcome before returning to awareness.

Our relationships with ourselves can also affect our relationship with nature. Again, the type of holding relationship that we form depends upon the attributes that we have rejected and now seek through the world of nature. If we are unaware of our inner power, we may try to find it through our attempts to dominate the external world. Some people use the traditional Christian view that humankind is to have dominion over the world and animals as an excuse to rape the land and force animals to serve their own needs and pleasures. Rather than living in harmony with the planet and viewing animals as part of the family of beings, they try to restore their inner power by dominating nature.

Native Americans teach that we should live in harmony with the world, rather than try to control or dominate it. Kent Newburn in *The Wisdom of Native Americans* says that they consider "nature to be the measure of consummate beauty, and its destruction to be a sacrilege." He reported proudly showing some visiting Sioux chiefs' artwork at the Corcoran Art Gallery in Washington, D.C. The response of one of the chiefs to the masterpieces showed the disdain that he felt over the rape of nature in America. "Ah!" he exclaimed, "Such is the strange philosophy of the white man! He hews down the forest that has stood for centuries in its pride and grandeur, tears up the bosom of Mother Earth, and causes the silvery watercourses to waste and vanish away. He ruthlessly disfigures God's own pictures and monuments, and then daubs a flat surface with many colors, and praises his work as a masterpiece!"

Eastern religions also promote living in harmony with nature. They differ, however, in viewing nature as "Maya" or an illusion that veils ultimate reality and our connection with Universal Being. According to Huston Smith in *The World's Religions*, Buddha sees the world as a burning house that we need to escape, while Islam compares the world to "vegetation that will be quickly harvested or turned to straw."

Doubting the inner power and control of our Divine nature can leave us fearful of nature. Instead of viewing nature as a friend, we see it as a terrifying and destructive force. The open spaces of a canyon or the vastness of the ocean often expose our hidden vulnerabilities and our fear of being overwhelmed. Traditional Christianity may have unwittingly fostered such fears by depicting a wrathful God who uses nature to punish humankind. In contrast, Native Americans teach a love of nature and believe that Wakan, the Great Spirit, permeates all things and is the unifying force binding all life together. "The Lakota was a true naturalist," Chief Luther Standing Bear is reported by Kent Newburn to have said, "a lover of nature." He loved the earth and all things of the earth, and the attachment grew with age. The old people came literally to love the soil and they sat or reclined on the ground with a feeling of being close to a mothering power." Early forms of Hinduism worshipped natural forces, which they believed were endowed with spiritual power. They had great reverence for rivers, mountains, and animals. Even today, they bathe in the Ganges to cleanse themselves spiritually, and at death they return their ashes to this their most sacred river.

Our relationship with ourselves also determines the type of relationship that we have with God. Neale Donald Walsch in Communion with God discusses the ten illusions that we create in our minds that affect our experience of the Divine. A whole book could be written on the different types of holding relationships that we can form with God. Instead of uniting with the Divine, we distance ourselves and reject the attributes of our divine nature. We then form holding relationships with God based on the divine attributes that we have rejected. If we perceive that we are powerless, unworthy, or unlovable, we may form holding relationships with God in which we become a Divine Victim or Divine Martyr.

Divine Victims fail to see that rejection of the Divine and its many attributes is the root of their problems. Instead, they believe that not only the world but also God is against them. They view life through a cloud of pessimism that rains only on them. Their true rainbow is black and blue and brings only hurt throughout their lives. By placing the locus of their problems outside of them, Divine Victims cannot grow or resolve their troubles. In *Radical Forgiveness: Making Room for the Miracle,* Colin Tipping exposes the victim consciousness in our modern thinking. He speaks of our identification with the victim archetype.

Divine Martyrs believe they can unite with the Divine and restore their divine nature by sacrificing and suffering. Their plan of salvation is outward rather than inward and involves martyring themselves for the Divine and for other people. They believe that loving and putting others before themselves is holier than loving others as themselves. Divine martyrs in the Christian tradition maintain this belief despite the fact that it violates the most fundamental principle of love that Jesus taught in the New Testament. In Luke 10:27, Jesus says to love our neighbor as ourselves. To love others more than ourselves is as unbalanced as to love ourselves more than others. To love our neighbor as ourselves is the more balanced way of relating to others.

Our personality type can determine not only the holding relationships that we have with others, but also the one we have with the Divine. Performer and Achiever personalities can also form relationships with the Divine that involve doing good works. Having rejected such attributes as love, joy, peace, and so on, they try to secure these fruits of the Divine by doing good deeds in the world. Conformers often try to form a relationship with God that is based on following the rules, rituals, and laws of a church. By rigidly following these, they believe that they can unite with the Divine and restore their divine nature. Clinging-Vine personalities can become locked into seeing God as only a strong father figure there to protect them. They look for power, love, and strength outside of themselves in a transcendent God. As a result, they never rediscover the divine attributes that they have rejected within themselves. Dominators are susceptible to becoming involved in power struggles with God and in the church. They often run for offices within the church hierarchy so as to regain a sense of their power. This type of power is only fleeting and masks the presence of their real inner power.

A final type of holding relationship that we can have with God is based on whether we are focused on the masculine or feminine face of the Godhead. We split off the masculine and feminine sides of ourselves by consciously identifying with one and relegating the other to the unconscious part of our mind. Likewise, we split God into two faces and identify with one to the exclusion of the other. By focusing on only one of these faces, either the masculine or the feminine, we are at risk of developing and holding onto a distorted relationship with the Divine.

In comparison with Hinduism, Buddhism, and Native American religions, traditional Christianity tends to split off the feminine aspect of the Godhead in favor of the masculine. Since we can easily see this split within the Christian tradition, let's examine its effects there. Keeping in mind our previous definition of the ways in which the masculine principle differs from the feminine principle—doing vs. being in terms of activity, objective vs. subjective sense of time, and heart vs. head in terms of understanding—it is clear that the views of the Divine in the Old Testament are based primarily on the masculine principle. Here, we see a distorted relationship with the Divine developing when the masculine principle, or "head," is severed from the feminine, or heart."

This "head centered" masculine view of the Divine emphasizes following the commandments. It considers the Divine as a father who can be vengeful, wrathful, or jealous unless we follow the rules. Moreover, He demands obedience and punishes us when it is not forthcoming. Such a view of God resulted in the legalism observed by Jesus in the behavior of the Pharisees and Sadducees who attempted to make themselves holy by doing good works, following the law, and performing certain rituals. They appeased God with certain acts to avoid His anger. This behavior involved "doing" or masculine energy and the idea that one had to do something to gain God's approval, or at the very least, to divert His wrath. The Old Testament view of humanity's relationship with God involved separation, guilt, condemnation, and obedience. Humankind was considered too lowly for a real relationship with God. Indeed, the Old Testament states that we will die if we look at the face of God. God is wrathful, vengeful, jealous, and angry in the Old Testament.

With Jesus, there is a new understanding of the Divine and consequently, a change in our relationship to the Divine. Jesus introduced the feminine face of the Godhead. His view reflects the feminine principle, for He spoke of the heart of God, of the love and forgiveness of God. He criticized the "head" and the "doing" approach of the Pharisees and Sadducees that came from the masculine principle. In the story of Mary and Martha, we can see a shift in emphasis from "doing" (the masculine form of activity) to "receiving" and "being" (the feminine form of activity). Here, we see Martha busy with her serving duties and annoyed that Mary is enjoying herself listening to Jesus. Martha breaks into their discussion with an indignant, "Lord, dost thou not care that my sister hath left me to serve alone? Bid her therefore, that she helps me." But Jesus says to her, "Martha, Martha" saying her name twice, and thus, according to Jewish tradition, putting real emphasis on what is to follow— "thou art careful and troubled by many things." He then suggests that all of her "doing" is not as important as what Mary is "receiving" by strengthening her "good part." The New Testament here and elsewhere suggests that we need only open our heart to come close to the Divine.

Jesus also emphasized another aspect of our relationship to the Divine that is based on the feminine mode of activity. This type of activity involves waiting, letting nature take its course, opening, allowing, receiving, and letting go. Jesus stressed the importance of quiet contemplation and prayer in our relationship to the Divine. Prayer and contemplation involve the feminine mode of activity, for in both we are opening ourselves to God, sometimes receiving His Spirit and at other times, asking for help. Open attentiveness and receiving are also at the core of the feminine mode of understanding. We need to allow our hearts and minds to be open to receive the wisdom of the Divine into our conscious minds. Jesus put more emphasis on being led by the Divine than on following the letter of the law.

Jesus' Law of Forgiveness is also based on the feminine mode of activity and involves letting go. He emphasized that God forgives us and calls upon us to forgive others, as well as ourselves. He thus redefined our relationship with God as one based on forgiveness and redemption instead of condemnation and blame. It is a relationship of love and is rooted in the heart of the feminine principle. Jesus brought the heart of God or the feminine aspect of the Divine back into balance with the head of God or the masculine aspect of the Divine presented in the Old Testament. In Jesus' teachings, God is less an angry and frightening Father than a loving one. But instead of embracing Jesus' principle of forgiveness, many Christians continue to live in the Old Testament under the law of "an eye for an eye."

In summation, we can have holding relationships in every realm of our existence—the physical, the social, the psychological, and the spiritual. But none of them will unite us to the Divine within and its fruits. In fact, in most cases, our holding relationships actually increase what they attempt to stop. If we disconnect from our wholeness, feel anxiety, and incorporate drugs or food to decrease it, we will feel good, but only temporarily, for we will become fat or addicted with continued use. In turn this creates more separation from our wholeness, more anxiety, and a greater sense of unworthiness, unlovability, or powerlessness. So, the holding relationships that we form fail and fail miserably to unite us with the Divine and restore the rejected attributes of our divine nature. Instead, these holding relationships hardened our hearts and block the Divine within from our conscious awareness.

Our holding relationships with ourselves and the external world of people, things, and actions are important only in that they show us what we need to do to clean and clear our hardened hearts and restore their purity in order to reconnect with the Divine within us. To undo a holding relationship, we must first become aware of the type of holding that we are caught in because that determines how we free ourselves. Although the techniques to undo holding relationships differ in form depending upon which realm, physical, social, psychological, or spiritual they deal with they are all based on the same principle. In the next chapter we will examine the basic principle that allows us to quickly undo the holding relationships that are producing our hardened hearts.

# Chapter 3
## THE FORGIVING HEART

**Be still, and know that I am God.**
**Psalm 46:10**

In the last chapter, we saw that a hardened heart is composed of all types of holding relationships we form to fill the void created when we separated ourselves from the Divine within us. In Matthew 5:8, we are told to give up our hardened hearts and have "pure" hearts. The Greek word for "pure" is *katharos,* which means a clear, clean, and unspoiled heart (*Hebrew-Greek Keyword Study Bible KJV* by Spiros Zodhiates, Th.D. and Warren Baker, D.R.E). But is there a specific spiritual technique that will clean and clear our hardened hearts? Yes, there is such a technique, and it involves the use of a very simple spiritual principle or law that can accomplish this mighty feat of cleansing our hardened hearts. This technique is stated in Psalm 46:10 where it says, "Be still, and know that I am God." According to the *Hebrew-Greek Keyword Study Bible KJV,* the Hebrew word "rap" means to be still, to relax, to cease, and to let go.

The activity of being still or letting go is just another way of talking about the Law of Forgiveness that Jesus introduced during His ministry. It took over thirty years for me to discover the importance of forgiveness in healing and undoing holding relationships. Actually, it was not so much a discovery of something brand new as it was a growing awareness that an existing principle had broader applications. The concept of forgiveness within Christianity has been narrowly focused and maintained as a strict dogma that has paradoxically been used to judge and condemn people of other faiths. Traditional Christianity discussed the importance of forgiveness mostly in terms of healing our relationships with God and others. It asserts that we have to accept Jesus' blood sacrifice before God will extend forgiveness to us and restore our relationship with Him. Some denominations of Christianity display as much fervor as militant Islam in condemning as infidels those who do not accept this tenet.

Close examination of the activity of religious sacraments, objects, or rituals that facilitate a union with the Divine, reveal that they are all based on the principle of forgiveness or letting go. The sacrament serves as a symbol for us to let go and join the Divine. "Almost anything can help us connect with sacred love or power," writes McColman, "if only we cultivate an open heart and a willing mind." Of course, we achieve both of these by applying the Law of Forgiveness and letting go of the thoughts in our minds and the hardness in our hearts.

McColman points out that many religions have such sacraments. Native Americans such as the Lakota offer the "sacred pipe to the Great Mystery." Reciting the "Diamond Sutra" in Buddhism is considered a sacramental act just as reading the Torah is in Judaism. Confirmation, baptism, and Holy Communion are similar sacraments that occur within the Christian tradition to let go of the past in order to be reborn into a new life more connected with the Divine. By examining the healing techniques of many religious faiths, as well as those associated withvarious psychological theories, I realized that they were all merely different applications of the basic Law of Forgiveness or letting go. In light of the realization that the majority of tools used by psychologists are based on the Law of Forgiveness introduced by Jesus, I found it very puzzling that many of the fundamental minsters that I see on TV actually condemned psychologists and their tools of healing. The process of letting something go to restore health and wholeness is the same whether it is used to heal a relationship, to let go of stress in the body or thoughts in the mind, or to have an experience of the Divine. This recognition led me to the conclusion that the Law of

Forgiveness has much broader applications than those proposed by traditional Christianity. Just as Gerald Jampolsky in *Forgiveness: The Greatest Healer of All* and Hugh Prather in *The Little Book of Letting Go* recently stated forgiveness is fundamental to all healing and health.

My journey in understanding this broader application of the Law of Forgiveness started with a search for ways to cope with the stress of everyday life. I began with the study of basic relaxation and meditation techniques. At first, I concentrated on the bodily relaxation techniques discussed by Edmund Jacobson in his 1938 book *Progressive Relaxation*. Jacobson called his method progressive relaxation training, and it involved the now familiar approach of reducing muscle tension by alternately tightening and relaxing various groups of muscles. The tightening phase helps us become consciously aware of our muscle tension while the relaxing phase involves directing our muscles to let go. This technique not only reduces our physical and emotional symptoms of stress, it also increases our energy and promotes a sense of well-being.

From Jacobson, I went on to the work of Walter Cannon and Hans Selye, who dealt with the importance of the autonomic nervous system in stress as well as in bodily disease and disorder. Cannon called the autonomic nervous system the fight/flight nervous system because it prepares us to either fight or flee from a threatening situation. We manifest stress in our bodies in different ways based on the type of autonomic nervous system activity triggered and the part of the body that it affects. We conceptualize the physical changes in our bodies produced by the autonomic nervous system as emotions.

The pioneering work of Cannon and Selye contributed not only to the development of psychosomatic medicine but also to the use of biofeedback in the treatment of stress related disorders. Biofeedback is what its name implies: a technique that gives us concrete feedback on what our body is doing. The feedback can be from muscle tension, heart rate, blood pressure, temperature, skin sweat response, or brain wave activity. By becoming consciously aware of our bodily responses to stress, we can learn to change them and undo the effects of the autonomic nervous system. We have used biofeedback on ourselves if we have ever taken our temperature or weighed ourselves. The thermometer tells us whether we are running a fever and the scales whether we have gained weight. Both devices "feed back" information about our body's condition. Armed with this information, we can take steps to change and improve our physical condition. When we're running a fever, we go to bed and drink fluids. When we've gained weight, we resolve to eat less—and sometimes we do.

Similarly, biofeedback machines are used to register changes in our internal bodily functions, but with far greater sensitivity and precision. This information is then used to teach us how to alter our brain activity, blood pressure, heart rate, and other bodily processes. By helping us to let go of the physical changes produced by stress, biofeedback training can restore bodily relaxation and harmony. In time, I realized that progressive relaxation, biofeedback, and similar relaxation procedures all involve the process of "letting go" in the physical realm. They apply the Law of Forgiveness or "letting go" to the muscles, organs, and autonomic nervous system in our bodies, thereby reducing stress and restoring a peaceful state. However, I discovered a problem with these strategies for undoing stress when I became aware they only deal with an effect. That is, they teach us how to let go of stress in our bodies but do not treat the source of the stress. Indeed, I realized that the real source of stress is in the mind and that the autonomic nervous system merely translates it into the body. If we think fearful, angry, or depressed thoughts, the autonomic nervous system becomes mobilized and translates these thoughts into bodily changes. We interpret these changes as emotions. Although physical relaxation techniques do produce significant changes in the body by teaching us how to let bodily stress go, they do not deal with the thinking that creates the stress responses in the first place.

As a result of this discovery, I shifted gears and began searching for techniques to deal with the mental causes of bodily stress. Interestingly enough, I soon realized that the various techniques to undo the cognitive or mental sources of stress are also different applications of the same basic Law of Forgiveness or "letting go." My search revealed that relaxation techniques, which included a mental component, were first popularized in the United States in the late 1960s. This came about when the Indian teacher, Maharishi Mahesh Yogi, promoted transcendental Meditation—a technique that focuses the mind on a mantra or personal sound to the exclusion of everything else. This technique works to clear the mind but holding any mental image to the exclusion of everything else works just as well. Holding a single thing within our minds, be it a point of light or a single sound, is called a one-pointed concentration technique, and the state of mind that we achieve is called one-pointed concentration.

The one-pointed concentration technique was a very important tool for me at the time. It taught me how to focus my mind by letting go of streams of thoughts. Through the years, I have noticed when my patients first begin trying to relax, they also encounter an undisciplined, rapid flow of thoughts and cannot sustain their focus. I have found a simple thought-stopping technique to be very helpful in disciplining and quieting the mind. When an unwanted thought appears, the technique involves first taking a deep breath. Thinking and breathing seem to be related, and breathing deeply can make a distracting thought disappear. After we breathe in, we should think "Stop!" and then let the thought go from our minds. Remember that we do not have to respond to a thought just because it appears in our minds. In fact, if we grab hold of a negative thought it will branch out like the roots of a tree into many other associated thoughts that can potentially lead us to deeper levels of stress.

Once we attain a state of one-pointed concentration, we easily realize how we have been possessed by our thoughts in the past. We can see how they pull us hither and yon, distracting us and stressing us. Like puppets, we danced to the thoughts appearing in our minds. By disciplining our minds to one-pointed concentration, we can go from being possessed by our thoughts to controlling when we think, what we think, and where we think. Then, we have thoughts, they do not have us. By applying the Law of Forgiveness, we are following the scripture "Be still, and know that I am God" (Psalm 46:10).

After transcendental meditation was introduced into this country, many other relaxation procedures were developed that combine both physical and mental techniques to reduce stress. On such technique, developed by J. H. Schultz, is called "Autogenic Training." Autogenic training uses not only tension and relaxation of muscles, but also mental images to accomplish relaxation. Shultz demonstrates that by holding a mental image in our mind, we can change the physical functioning of our body. For example, if we hold a picture of a lemon in our mind long enough, we will begin to salivate. Our body does not know whether the lemon is in our mind, in our mouth, or lying on a table, but it salivates just the same.

The relaxation and meditation techniques I studied not only helped me to have mentally and physically rejuvenating experiences, they also opened my awareness to other levels of consciousness I wanted to explore. Consequently, I began reading extensively in Eastern religions, especially in Zen Buddhism, and most especially the works of D. T. Suzuki. Overall, my focus was on achieving a quiet mind, but now, I also wanted to experience oneness with the universe as opposed to living in what Eastern religions call the subject-object dichotomy.

The subject-object dichotomy refers to the schism between the world and ourselves. The idea behind the term is that thinking separates us from unity within ourselves and with the universe. In order to think about something, we have to distinguish ourselves from the thing we are thinking about. Thinking separates us as the "thinking subject" from the object of our thoughts, and results in the subject-object dichotomy. Meditation and koans are cardinal techniques used by Zen Buddhism to break the subject-object dichotomy and lead one into a state of "satori," enlightenment, or union with the "Being" of the universe. Zen meditation typically involves sitting in a cross-legged position, hands joined, eyes open and looking down. The meditating person then tries to let all thoughts in the mind go through one-pointed concentration until reaching satori. This is a clear application of the Law of Forgiveness to quieten the mind and body.

Koans are used in conjunction with meditation to confound the logical thinking of the rational mind. These are paradoxical statements that cannot be understood with ordinary logic. For example, the question, "What is the sound of one hand clapping?" defies the rational mind, forces a person to let go of the subject-object dichotomy to find

33

an answer, and thereby induces a state of satori. The koans show the limits of the analytical and logical left side of the brain and can only be solved by moving more into the intuitive right side of the brain.

I also discovered that other religions of the East have techniques to awaken different types of consciousness and achieve experiences of wholeness and pure being. In Hinduism, different forms of yoga are practiced in order to achieve higher states of consciousness and experiences of union. In fact, the word "yoga" means the experience of union with the universe. Training in yoga involves rigorous exercises in diet, posture, reading, intellectual concentration, and moral discipline to overcome the blocks of our lower nature and thereby enable us to enter into the state of samadhi—a word that both Buddhists and Hindus use to refer to the state of mystical consciousness. Like many medieval Christian monks and hermits living in caves, Buddhists and some sects of Hinduism use sensory and sleep deprivation, fasting, and meditative techniques to unlock the mind, break the subject-object dichotomy, enter the "void of nothingness" and then Nirvana, a mystical state of union with the universe.

Along with studying Eastern religions, I started meditating on a daily basis. I began entering deeper and deeper levels of the mind by letting go of my rational thinking and its stream of associations in my conscious mind. Then one evening, I had an experience that abruptly changed my behavior. It was an experience of nothingness. It began as a feeling, not just an intellectual conclusion, of being only a minute grain of sand in a vast and overwhelming universe. This sense of insignificance left me feeling isolated and alone. I felt dark and empty inside. This experience was frightening and I immediately stopped the daily meditation. Later, I learned that what I had stumbled upon was not unique. It is called the "Great Emptiness" and fear is a common response to it. As a result of this experience, I stopped not only meditating but also reading in Eastern religions. I was glad at the time that I could switch the focus of my energies on to getting my master's degree and take a breather from my search.

As I reflected on my experiences, it became clear to me that my search for ways to cope with the stress of everyday living had changed from the physical to the mental realm. I was now exploring the mind and searching for ways to relax it. Meditation had shown me ways to remove stress by letting go of my thoughts so as to achieve one-pointed concentration. I also realized that like physical relaxation techniques, cognitive and meditation techniques are also applications of the Law of Forgiveness or letting go but differ in being applied to the mental realm.

Still frightened by the results of my journey through Eastern religious thinking, I decided now to look into my own spiritual backyard for some answers. I was brought up in the Christian faith, so that is where I focused my attention. I began attending church frequently and reading religiously, you might say. At one time during this phase of my search, I met weekly with three different ministers from three different denominations to learn more about Christianity. At this time, I was struck by Christianity's emphasis on love, forgiveness, and experiencing a personal relationship with God that was almost absent in Eastern religious thinking. Although some sects of Hinduism also believe that liberation can be obtained by a personal, loving relationship with the Divine, Buddhism rejects this and also the performance of religious rituals as a means to achieve release from the world. Awareness of a loving relationship with the Divine did, however, help ease my fear of being nothing in a vast unknowable universe. My studies further revealed that the subject-object dichotomy discussed in many Eastern religions could also be found in Christian teachings. The story in Genesis about eating the fruit of the tree of knowledge of good and evil implies that it caused humankind to develop a split, dualistic mind which led to separation from God. Within Christianity, the dichotomy between good and evil receives more emphasis, but like Eastern religions, it also suggests that this dualistic knowledge produces a separation from God.

At the same time that I began reading exclusively in Christianity, I was studying logic and the philosophy of science in graduate school. In particular, I was caught up in thoughts about the principle of causality—the core of the scientific method—which maintains that every effect has a cause. For example, if we strike a match, the fire is the effect and the strike is the cause. I then applied the principle of causality to my religious thinking and concluded that without the concept of God as

First Cause, our whole system of logical thinking about the way the world operates is invalid. I reasoned that if we apply the principle of cause and effect to the natural world and trace it back to the beginning of time and don't postulate God as Prime Cause, then we have an effect without a cause. This causeless effect invalidates our logical assumption that the principle of causality operates in the world of nature. Of course, if we do postulate God, then God becomes the causeless effect and this would similarly invalidate the whole system of logic. Yet most religions view the Divine as a causeless cause. Within the Christian tradition, we are told in Exodus 3:14 that God said of himself, "I am that I am…".

During the next decade, I continued studying Christianity, philosophy, and psychology. During most of this period I was preparing for my doctoral orals, and I did my studying at Lake Waco. My philosophical studies helped me understand my metaphysical assumptions about the universe. Specifically, they helped me realize that everything is an assumption. People who do not believe in the existence of God often say that if you can't sense the Divine in the finite world then it means that He is not real and does not exist. They point to nature and say that it can be experienced; and therefore, it is real and does exist. From these studies, I came to see that scientists really operate on faith as much as theologians. They base their systems on the assumption that the external world is real. What an insight it was for me at the time to realize that scientists also operate on the basis of faith. But more important to my search was the idea that the external world is an assumption and not ultimate reality. My early Christian upbringing had taught me that the world was real and created by God. But like the adherents of many Eastern religions, I now believed that the world of nature was not just an assumption but an illusion, or "Maya", through which we pass to ultimate reality, our destination.

Around this time, I began having religious experiences at the lake that included several new aspects ushered in by my recent insights. I had learned with the physical relaxation procedures how to let my body and emotions go and I could empty my mind with the thought-stopping technique so as to achieve one pointed concentration. But now I could use these techniques of letting go while walking around in the world. I also realized why some denominations in Christianity, as well as Sufi, a mystical branch of Islam, and Native American religions incorporate dance into their worship.

Physical activity, like silence, can also serve as a way to let go of our holding relationships and open to an experience of the Divine. I viewed nature through the lens of my new insights and saw it as a beautiful, but illusory veil covering the Divine. I then let go of my sense of separation from this veil and joined with it. As I let go more and more, I experienced the light of the Divine. I began not only to see light in the world of nature, but also to feel its glow within my own body. It was as if the light from the candle in my prior dream and its associated loving feeling was permeating everything. And as I looked outward into the world a golden light reflected gently off everything I saw. It was like the glistening reflection seen at sunset and daybreak. Inwardly, I experienced the light as a loving feeling and felt a connection to its source. The experience felt like leaving a flat, three-dimensional world and entering a world of depth with many dimensions glistening with sunlight and love.

Unfortunately, I started having such intense experiences of the Divine that I again, lost my nerve and became frightened. At this time, my thoughts centered on the similarities between my experiences and those of psychotics. This alarmed me to the point that on one occasion I snatched my belongings, literally ran to my car, and fled the lake. When I later told the rector of my church about these experiences and my misgivings about them, he assured me that such experiences were unusual but not necessarily abnormal. He suggested I read William James' *Varieties of Religious Experiences* and some of Carl Jung's psychodynamic work. I had not read the work of James or Jung at any length but now dipped into their writings. In William James' book, I discovered that perfectly sane people had experienced the same things as I, and this comforted me. Carl Jung's psychodynamic work provided me with some new healing techniques and some new theoretical concepts that were crucial in understanding my past experiences.

In Jung's work, I found two important tools: dream analysis and active imagination. These helped me become conscious of personality factors that block religious experiences and need to be undone. Jung saw dreams as X-rays of the mind. The trick is to learn how to interpret what a dream means. Active imagination is a technique for actively holding dream contents in the mind while in a relaxed but awakened state and observing how they change and what they do. By using these techniques, we can gain an awareness of the negative mental contents that need to be undone if we are to experience the Divine within us.

Carl Jung's concept of the "Self Archetype" helped me understand my prior experiences and ultimately experiencing the Divine. Jung postulated the concept of the Self as the true center of the mind. He believed that we are born with this unifying principle and it serves to integrate experiences and bring wholeness to our minds. This led me to the conclusion that my unusual experiences could well be encounters with the Self, and as such those of wholeness, not craziness, as I had originally feared. Jung's concept of the Self seemed to be like the Hindu notion of "atman" or the eternal within man, which is a part of the "Great Soul" that undergirds the universe.

In *Story Keepers A Journey into Native American Spirituality,* John James Stewart reports a legend told by the Ojibwa Tribe to account for why it is hard to be wise. The Creator goes to the animals on Earth and announces that He is creating a new Two-Legged creature but plans to hide the two qualities—Wisdom and Justice— that it needs to become whole and live in harmony with all animals on Earth. Only a tiny mole offers an acceptable solution to the Creator. The mole suggested that the two virtues be hidden within the Two-Legged creature itself since "to look inward is one of the hardest things to do" thus "only the most perceptive of the Two-Leggeds will be able to discover these wonderful gifts."

I then wondered if the concept of the Self could be found within Christian teachings so I begin to search the Bible for an answer. There, I found a number of passages supporting the idea of a Divine spark within us. The statement in Genesis 1:26-27 that tells us, "God created man in his own image" suggests to me the creation of an imminent God within each of us. In Jeremiah 31:33, we see, "But this shall be the covenant that I will make with the house of Israel: After those days, saith the Lord, I will put my law in their inward parts, and write it in their hearts, and will be their God and they shall be my people." The Hebrew word for heart is leb, which is used as a noun referring to the immaterial inner self or being. The teachings of the "I AM" by Helen Blavatsky, C.G. Ballard and his wife, and Geraldine Innocent used the term I AM Presence to refer to the Divine spark within us. This immanent God within, or Imago Deo, seems to me to be the place where we unite with the Divine and again, experience ourselves as "children of the Highest." It is our door into eternity. It is what Meister Eckhart, a Christian mystic during the Middle Ages, meant when he said, "the eye with which I see God is the same eye with which God sees me." Eckhart likens this experience of God to that of hearing an echo: "It is," he says, "as if one stood before a high mountain and cried, "Art thou there"' and God's echo returns, Art thou there?' And it is exactly here that we can experience the Divine within.

Another avenue that I followed while reading the works of Jung involved the issues of masculinity and femininity. This excursion served to clarify the principle of forgiveness, the key concept I found to be behind all healing methods. At this time the women's movement was in full swing, but I did not really feel comfortable with some of the ideas that I was hearing from its camp. These women seemed to me to be rejecting such manifestations of the feminine principle as homemaking and motherhood in favor of others such as working in the world and being an independent, strong, and Amazonian type of woman. In order to resolve this conflict, I began reading extensively in the writings of various Jungian analysts who dealt with issues of masculinity and femininity.

According to Jungian theory, the masculine principle differs from the feminine principle in terms of activity, time perception, and type of understanding. The masculine mode of activity is of an initiating, arousing, erecting, and generating nature. It is assertive in that it moves toward a goal. This type of activity can easily be seen on a fundamental biological level in the behavior of sperm, which flips its tail to initiate headlong movements toward the ova to initiate conception. On a much larger scale, the same type of goal-directed activity can be seen in a man.

He will actively change the environment and make consciously thought-out plans to achieve his goals. The feminine mode of activity, however, is open, receptive, and yielding. It involves opening to a process, waiting, and attending to things. This mode of activity is containing, receiving, and being—and it is also clearly evident in a woman's basic reproductive behavior. She must be open and receptive to the swimming sperm in order to achieve conception. The ovum awaits the penetration of the sperm.

The masculine and feminine principles also differ in terms of their orientation to time. The masculine mode of experiencing time is quantitative. It is objective and clock-like. It focuses on the past, present, and future. The feminine mode of time is experienced as qualitative rather than quantitative. It is subjective, personal, and rhythmic, a waxing and waning. And again the biology of women reflects this waxing and waning rhythm of time in the menstrual cycle.

A third difference between the masculine and feminine principles is in their modes of understanding. The masculine mode is objective, head-centered, and analytical. Its approach to solving problems is to objectively view the pertinent facts, then reach logical conclusions from them. The feminine mode is heart-centered, subjective, and intuitive. A woman conceives or gives birth to an idea or thought in her conscious mind often without any awareness that she was searching for a solution to a problem at all. As you have probably guessed, the feminine mode understanding is often called woman's intuition.

While I was thinking about the masculine and the feminine principles (doing vs. being, objective vs. subjective time, and head vs. heart understanding) in my mind, I turned back to my Christian readings and saw them in a new light. Like McColman, I began to see that the Divine "is a full manifestation of both masculine and feminine qualities." Moreover, the revelation of God and our relationship to Him as presented in the Old Testament now appeared to me to be based primarily on the masculine principle. During Old Testament times, the emphasis was on taking a head-centered, masculine approach to God. God was understood as a Father who could be vengeful, wrathful, and jealous when his rules or commandments were violated. Additionally, the masculine principle of "doing" was necessary to gain God's approval, or at the least to ward off His wrath. Humankind's relationship with God was characterized by separation, guilt, condemnation, and obedience.

As I read the teachings of Jesus in the light of Jungian thinking, I saw that He created a profound shift in our understanding of the nature of God and in our relationship to Him. It now seemed clear to me that Jesus had introduced the feminine face of the Godhead. In chastising the legalism of the Pharisees and Sadducees, He was criticizing the head-only approach of the masculine principle. When He commanded us to love God and each other (Matthew 22:37-40), He was actually transforming all the laws and commandments of the Old Testament into a single law of love, a law of the heart, a law based on the feminine principle. Additionally, the feminine mode of open attentiveness and waiting is essential to having religious experiences. To experience the presence of the Divine, we must wait patiently and open our hearts. Prayer also involves this form of feminine activity. In prayer, we are opening ourselves to God, sometimes in contemplation, and other times to ask for help.

Finally, and most importantly for our purposes, I came to realize that the Law of Forgiveness that Jesus introduced also involves the feminine mode of activity which is letting go, being, and receiving. The feminine mode of understanding allows us to focus on, or open our hearts to, the guidance of the Divine. Such a focus allows the wisdom of God to be born into our conscious minds. So, with Jesus' teachings, we see a shift from a head-centered approach to God that requires following the commandments of an angry, frightening Father, to a heart-centered approach to a forgiving and loving Father.

Many Christians still live in Moses' Old Testament world of law and punishment, rather than in Jesus' New Testament world of love and forgiveness. I believe Jesus' Law of Forgiveness, which is based on the feminine principle, is the real essence of his revelation in re-establishing our union with God. This idea was confirmed for me when I read *A Course in Miracles*, which considers forgiveness to be a defense of letting go that ultimately points us back to God. From my Sunday school days, I had believed forgiveness meant I sat on my lofty throne of moral elevation and dispensed unmerited pardon to miserable people who had wronged me. I once thought of forgiveness only in terms of forgiving another person but now, I realized forgiveness really means letting go and has a much broader application than simply forgiving others. *A Course in Miracles* views forgiveness as the one means of defending ourselves against misfortunes because it does not create any other problems and always reconnects us with the Divine.

As I pondered the idea that forgiveness is simply a process of letting go of something, I realized that the healing techniques that I had been studying and using on myself and others over the years were merely different applications of this one basic Law of Forgiveness. All relaxation techniques, whether they focus on the physical realm, the mental realm, or both, are different manifestations of the same principle of letting go, or forgiveness. In the physical realm, we relax by letting the muscles and organs of our bodies go in biofeedback and other relaxation techniques. In the mental realm, we can achieve a relaxed mind by using the techniques from the Eastern religions that involve letting go of our thoughts. Although there are diverse ways to conceptualize the workings of the mind and many tools to reveal its contents, healing still comes by applying the principle of forgiveness and letting go of any disturbing mental processes. In the spiritual realm, we let go of our holding relationships or attachments to the world of people, things, and actions in order to achieve a union with the Divine. Even though Jesus introduced forgiveness as a tool to reunite with the Divine, traditional Christianity, as well as Judaism and Islam, believe that our ego attachments can only be controlled, not completely overcome. Buddhism and Hinduism differ in believing that these attachments can be completely undone.

I now knew that systematically applying the Law of Forgiveness would reconnect me with the Divine within, and I did not need a lot of abstract philosophy or countless theories to achieve such a mystical experience. All I need to know at any one time is which holding relationship is blocking my connection to the Divine within and which form of forgiveness I must use to undo the block. Sometimes, I imagine this process as working like a computer with a number of programs operating. The one we have open and are working on is in the foreground—like our conscious mind. The many programs operating in the background are like our unconscious mind. Now let's assume that the Divine or Imago Deo program lies behind all of these other programs and at the center of our hard drive. In order to open the "Self" program and place it on our desktop, we must find the programs that are blocking or conflicting with it and close them out. We must bring them to the foreground—to the conscious mind—in order to close or delete them so they do not prevent the "Self" program from operating properly. The delete key is like the principle of forgiveness. We can use this key to undo the interfering programs that are blocking our awareness or access to the Divine or Imago Deo program stored on the hard disc.

With the Law of Forgiveness, I had the right concept to undo the holding relationships in my hardened heart, but now, I needed to determine which tool or form of forgiveness to use on any given occasion to achieve the experience. I discovered that the type of forgiveness needed depends upon which realm of being—physical, mental, spiritual, or some combination of these—contained the holding relationship that was blocking awareness of the Divine. In the physical realm, the principle of forgiveness or letting go is essential for the proper functioning of the body although we are mostly unaware of this.

Letting go serves as the basis for our movements and our ability to sense the external world. We could not even move around unless we let go of our muscles in one position and contract muscles in another position. To visually scan a room, we have to let go of what we are currently looking at before we can focus on something else in our visual field. In both cases, we give a direction to our muscles and senses to let go of something in order to do something else. We have practiced letting go on the physical level so much that the process becomes automatic and we don't even think about it. The basic act of moving is an application of the principle of forgiveness at the most fundamental level of our existence. Only when a holding pattern in our bodies becomes fixed, rigid, or painful from disease or disorder do we become aware that the principle of forgiveness or letting go is no longer operating properly. Thus, it hardly seems strange that the healing of these fixed and rigid physical patterns come from the application of forgiveness or letting them go in the body. We are simply restoring what was lost. Examination of the relaxation, meditation, and biofeedback techniques discussed earlier in this chapter reveal that they are all based on letting go of the body, its nerves, muscles, and organs in order to restore free flowing harmony and peace.

Robin Casarjian in *Forgiveness: A Bold Choice for a Peaceful Heart* details how she uses the principle of forgiveness to heal a negative holding relationship with our body. She combines word association and affirmation work to identify hidden thoughts and feelings about our body. By making them conscious, she maintains that we can let these thoughts and feelings go and then cultivate a more positive view of our body. She then suggests an exercise involving expressing gratitude as a powerful tool to develop love and acceptance of our body.

With the idea that the Law of Forgiveness was paramount in the healing process, I began my internship in the mid-1980s at a pain clinic in Dallas, Texas. I designed a pain program using the different applications of the principle of forgiveness that included the relaxation, imaging, and autogenic techniques I had studied. With these techniques I was able to help many patients manage their pain and reduce their use of pain medications. However, I noticed that most patients did not understand either the emotional or the cognitive component involved in their pain. They displayed little knowledge of any relationship between their minds and their bodies. At the beginning of a therapy session, I would ask patients about their pain since I had last seen them. Generally, they would respond that the pain was high, but they were unaware of what might have caused it to increase, particularly when the cause was psychological. To help them understand the relationship between mind and body, I recalled Freud's free association technique.

Freud observed that when patients lying on a couch were allowed to talk about whatever came to mind, they usually zeroed in on what was bothering them. I wondered if this technique could be used in the body to uncover repressed material associated with states of inflation and deflation. I started experimenting with it in the body and eventually developed the procedure I call "Somatic Free Association." This technique entails focusing awareness on the pain or disorder in the body and then allowing the thoughts behind the bodily problem to come back into full consciousness. I was essentially teaching patients how to use free association to uncover their holding relationships with their bodies and find the psychological factors that were causing their physical pain. Once the person became aware of the holding relationship with the body that was associated with their pain, the Law of Forgiveness could be applied to let it go and thus decrease their pain.

Very simply, the somatic free association technique entails focusing awareness on the pain or disorder in the body and then allowing the thoughts behind the bodily problem to come back into full consciousness. The "focusing of awareness" part of the procedure involves concentrating on the sensations arising from the problem area of the body and then experiencing them fully. Next the patient formulates a question directed inward and intended to reveal the unconscious thoughts and feelings behind the pain and bodily disorders. For example, the patient might ask, "How do I feel hurt?" or "What have I done to hurt myself?" He or she then must be quiet and attend or listen to whatever surfaces in response to this question, just as one would listen to a friend having a problem.

If we follow this procedure and are not afraid of what might come up, our quiet letting go and listening will allow the thoughts and feelings behind our bodily problems to surface into awareness. This technique differs from the way we typically deal with problems in everyday life because it does not involve actively analyzing reasons behind our bodily upsets. Rather, the somatic free association technique is a form of listening and experiencing to get at the thoughts and feelings hidden behind disease or pain in the body.

To illustrate how somatic free association actually works, let's examine some situations where it proved to be helpful to my patients in healing holding relationships with the body. A number of years ago, I had a patient, who for her age, had many medical problems that were interfering with her ability to maintain employment. Her psychological testing indicated that her emotional problems were exacerbating her medical situation. During one session she complained that she always had a hard knot in the upper left side of her back around the third or fourth thoracic vertebrae. When relaxation exercises proved ineffective, I tried somatic free association to discover if any psychological dynamics might be behind the trouble. I explained the procedure to her and then walked her through it. To our mutual surprise, a thirty-five-year-old memory fully explaining why she was holding in this area of her body popped into her consciousness during the first session. She remembered being about five years old and walking down some steps into the basement of her home. Her mentally disturbed mother was behind her and tried to kill her by pushing her down the stairs. She could again feel her mother's hand shoving against the very part of her back that was now in pain. This traumatic memory had been pushed into unconsciousness, but it continued to make itself felt through a knotting of the muscles. The patient was, as the expression goes, still holding on for dear life. After we dealt with this terrifying memory, she was able to let it go, and the muscles of her back also unknotted and relaxed.

In another striking instance, somatic free association revealed a deadly disease in a pain patient. During my internship at the pain clinic, I conducted nightly group therapy sessions, and one of my exercises used somatic free association. Each patient was instructed to feel his or her pain and then let it open up and reveal what would make it feel better. Since some patients viewed this technique as a little weird, I also offered the option of imaging a pain box, opening it, and seeing what was inside. This more concrete version of somatic free association proved more acceptable to some patients but still revealed underlying psychological dynamics associated with many pain problems. A 58-year-old man in the group saw only a half circle in his pain box. When he reported this image during the discussion part of the group session, Jung's concept of the mandala or circle that represents wholeness leaped into my mind. A half circle, I thought, might imply that the patient's wholeness had somehow been breached or broken. I did not mention the interpretation at the time because the idea of broken wholeness struck me as serious, and I wanted more information before revealing it. The following night when I returned to the clinic, I found my intuition about the seriousness of the image confirmed. Another patient caught me as I was getting on the elevator and told me that this patient had been diagnosed with terminal cancer and sent to another hospital. The broken wholeness that somatic free association had revealed through the patient's half-circle image had been revelatory indeed.

I have also used somatic free association on myself and been equally impressed at its ability to reveal psychological conflicts hidden behind physical ills. After I completed my internship in the Pain Program at Dallas Rehabilitation Institute, I was hired as director of the pain program. In the process of closing down my old office, I begin to feel tightness in the upper part of my chest and suspected that I was about to get an upper respiratory infection. When I arrived at the hospital with some of my things, a nurse stopped me and said that the blood work they required me to have indicated my white count was higher than normal. I told her that I was getting ready to have an upper respiratory infection. Sure enough, that evening my temperature shot up and I got so sick that I took some antibiotics. While sitting on my balcony later that weekend, I grew curious about what was behind my illness and decided to use the somatic free association technique to uncover any psychological dynamics that might be causing it. I began by bringing the pain in my upper chest into my awareness and allowing myself to fully feel the uncomfortable sensations there. I then asked myself, "What is causing the problem?" and listened quietly for a response from within. After a while a sense of fear began to creep over me, and gradually I realized that I was afraid of failing in my new endeavor. I could now use the cognitive-feeling techniques to uncover and let go of the thinking that was producing the fear and ultimately the disorder in my body. I discovered that I was afraid of being hurt by the loss of self-esteem or worthiness. By using the somatic free association technique, I had found the cause of my bodily disorder and now had a way to correct it at its source, by undoing the doubting thoughts in my mind.

Through somatic free association, I had found a way to help patients become consciously aware of what was behind their holding relationships with their bodies. With this technique, I could help them recognize the feelings and ultimately the thoughts behind their physical problems. I could then show them how to use the cognitive-feeling technique to undo their destructive feelings and thereby restore a healthy relationship with the body. In *The 5 Steps to Achieve Healing*, Jacques Martel describes 5 steps to achieve healing in the body that include knowledge, openness, letting go, acceptance, and action. He maintains that we can heal our bodies by practicing these 5 steps. Note that his steps do include letting go and acceptance both terms associated with the Law of Forgiveness.

Just as the Law of Forgiveness or letting go is crucial for the proper functioning of the body, it is necessary on the mental level for the smooth functioning of the mind. In order to concentrate and think clearly, we have to let go of intrusive or distracting thoughts. We also need to let go of thoughts about hurts, slights, and trauma stemming from other people or from present or past circumstances in our lives. Otherwise, our minds can become fixed and rigid with looping webs of negative thoughts that produce disease and disorder in our psyches and ultimately in our bodies. Again, it hardly seems strange that forgiveness brings about healing. It allows us to let go of these fixed thoughts that block the smooth functioning of our minds. I have already discussed several methods for letting go in the mind, such as the thought stopping technique and one-pointed concentration methods emphasized in Eastern religious thinking. All of the seemingly different healing techniques developed in psychology are based on making fixed and rigid patterns of thoughts and behaviors conscious, but we can only be healed of them by applying the principle of forgiveness and then letting them go. Although psychologists have not conceptualized their techniques this way, forgiveness is the underlying principle that brings about healing through letting go of some form of holding in the mind.

In recent years a number of techniques dealing with both the physical and mental realms and based on the concept of forgiveness have been introduced. Gerald Jampolsky, *in Forgiveness: The Greatest Healer of All*, focuses mostly on applying forgiveness to heal our relationships with others. His work is based primarily on *A Course in Miracles* and suggests a two-stage process of preparation and action to achieve forgiveness. In the preparation stage, we are instructed to develop a quiet, open mind through some form of meditation. In the action stage, we are encouraged to develop a "willingness" to turn over our grievances to a Higher Power. In *The Little Book of Letting Go*, Hugh Prather also proposes a mostly cognitive approach to forgiveness but has three rather than two steps in the letting go process. According to Prather, we must first determine what we think and feel about a block to our wholeness. Then we must develop a desire to let the block go. The final step according to Prather is to respond with our whole mind rather than with just our conflicted mind. We must find our place of wholeness from within and deal with the problem from this vantage point. In *Forgive for Good*, Fred Luskin discusses how grievances form and suggests using a combination of breathing, active imagination, and thought refocusing to undo them. He calls his plan PERT, or Positive Emotion Refocusing Technique. He maintains that PERT undoes each step involved in the formation of a grievance as well as the flight/fight response of the autonomic nervous system.

Colin Tipping, in *Radical Forgiveness: Making Room for the Miracle*, introduces a five-stage Radical Forgiveness technique to help undo our sense of victimhood. He mostly uses a cognitive approach but also suggests that "satori" breathwork is very helpful to integrate changes. Regardless of which method we choose to heal ourselves, they all represent some form of the principle of forgiveness or letting go to achieve this goal. This realization should help prevent the glorification of one healing tool to the exclusion of others. Instead, we can accept that certain healing methods will help some of us but not others.

We can undo our feelings of anxiety, anger, and depression by using what I call cognitive-feeling techniques. These tools reel in our projections so that we no longer see the world as the source of our emotional upsets. Cognitive-feeling techniques undo feelings by identifying and changing the thoughts behind them. Most of us deal with our feelings by using our thinking mode first. We use our thoughts to judge, deny, project, minimize, rationalize, or dismiss our feelings. But each of these strategies results in keeping our feelings and placing them in the basement of our minds or into our bodies. In *The Little*

*Book of Letting Go,* Hugh Prather presents a number of release exercises that involve cognitive techniques to let go of unwanted emotions. He suggests a type of free association in which we sit with our distressing emotion and write down any associated thoughts that surface in our mind. He believes that we need to find the "T-thoughts" that were formed early in life and produce emotions that block our wholeness. I have developed a cognitive-feeling technique that is more directive in that it asks specific questions so as to move us quickly from the emotional to the thought level. It involves first becoming aware of and accepting our feelings, then asking questions to move to the thinking level for understanding, and finally applying forgiveness and letting go. Let's now examine the steps involved in using this technique to deal with the emotion of anxiety.

Anxiety is a mild form of fear of being hurt in some way. When we feel anxious or when we notice that some part of our body is tense, we need to ask ourselves this question: In what way am I afraid of being hurt? Then we need to be quiet and listen for an answer from within. In our quiet contemplation we will discover that our anxiety is associated with a fear of being hurt by the loss of some aspect of our divine nature. We can be afraid that we will be hurt by the loss of love, joy, peace, control, power, meekness, goodness, patience, gentleness, faith, or some combination of these divine qualities. For example, when, we think that others may reject or abandon us, we are afraid of being hurt by the loss of love. When we fear being hurt by the loss of power or control our thoughts involve beliefs that we will be hurt when others take our power or control from us. We can be afraid of being hurt by the loss of goodness or worthiness. Here we are afraid that others who don't respect or see us as worthy will hurt us.

Once we identify the way in which we are afraid of being hurt, we leave the physical/emotional level, where we actually feel anxiety, and move to the cognitive level, where our thoughts about anxiety are located. Our awareness has moved from a mere feeling reaction to a discovery of the thoughts associated with what is happening in the outside world. It is our thoughts about what is happening that determine our emotions and need correcting. The good news here is that if we change the thoughts, then we also change the way we feel. It is at the thought level that we can control and undo our feelings.

Understanding the way we are afraid of being hurt determines how we need to correct our thinking to undo our fear. It reveals the aspect(s) of our divine nature that we have doubted in response to some person or situation and need to reaffirm. If the thoughts associated with our fears of being hurt by the loss of love, we need to let them go. Next we reaffirm our inner love by reminding ourselves that love is our gift from God and that nothing outside of ourselves can take it from us unless it is more powerful than God. In this way, we allow the love within us to resurface into our awareness. We use the same process to undo our fear of being hurt by the loss of power, self-esteem, or any of the fruits of our divine nature. We need to let go of such thoughts and then reaffirm what we have rejected from our awareness. In this way, we can reconnect with the Divine within us, and therefore with our divine nature. We may have to reaffirm the presence of what we have doubted many times because we tend to fall back into our old mental habits. Fear can now become a gauge that signals when we are not doing something that we need to do. For when we feel fear, we know that we are harboring thoughts of doubt that we need to let go in order to reunite with the Divine and restore the fruits of our divine nature.

Like anxiety, anger also revolves around hurts associated with the perceived loss of aspects of our divine nature. It is different from anxiety in that when we are angry, we are attacking such qualities as love, power, and worthiness instead of simply doubting them. And our minds are so powerful that if we attack aspects of our divine nature, then we feel weakened and lacking in these qualities. Most people are aware only of being angry, but thoughts of hurt are always lurking under anger. When we discover that we are angry or that anger is behind our bodily upsets, we should first allow ourselves to feel and accept our anger without judgment or justification.

When we are actually feeling the anger, we should then ask ourselves in what way we think that we have been hurt. We must then let ourselves sink into and feel the hurt underlying the anger. While experiencing the hurt, we need to ask ourselves in which way we feel hurt or which aspect of our divine nature do we believe has been weakened. Do we feel hurt by the loss of love, power, joy, self-esteem, and so on, or by some combination of these divine fruits? When we identify the type of hurt that we feel, we can become aware of the thoughts that produced them, and in some cases disorder in our bodies. Then we can let the attacking thoughts go. Finally, we reaffirm the qualities of our divine nature that we believed were weakened by our attacking thoughts. By letting these thoughts go and reaffirming our divine nature, we welcome our connection to the Imago Deo within, along with its many fruits.

To illustrate how anger occurs and how to use the cognitive-feeling technique to undo it, let me relate an experience that I had around the time that I was discovering this technique. In an automobile, I am a fast driver and occasionally alarm other drivers. Within the span of a month three different drivers gave me the finger on highways around Dallas. On the third occasion, I had somewhat too speedily left the freeway and pulled behind some cars waiting for a green light on the access road. While waiting for the light to change, I glanced at the car on my left, and the driver shot me the finger. I immediately felt a rush of anger, but as I clenched my jaw, I thought, "Linda, you need to deal constructively with this." So, rather than leaping out of my car and grabbing the offending driver by the necktie, I chose to use the cognitive-feeling technique.

I began by dealing with the emotional component and allowed myself to fully feel my anger without judgment or justification. Then I let the anger go and allowed myself to feel the hurt underlying the anger. While doing that, I asked myself, "In what way do you feel hurt by being given the finger?" As I sat there in the car, a feeling of hurt from the loss of love arose in my body. I felt hurt by the loss of love upon being given the finger by this driver.

Next, I used the cognitive part of the cognitive-feeling technique and challenged the absurd notion that someone's giving me the finger could diminish the love that God had given me. Of course, if this driver was more powerful than God then he could diminish all my God-given love and I would then be lacking in love. But another glance at the driver assured me that he was not more powerful than God, and so it was reasonable to assume that his finger-wagging behavior in no way changed me. And yet I did at this moment feel changed by the event because I felt hurt and anger. So, what had happened? If the driver could do nothing to change me, then the culprit must have been my own thoughts attacking me and leaving me feeling hurt and angry. Now I could use my mind to attack myself, but it would never bring me happiness or peace of mind. So, I let go of the thoughts causing my hurt and anger, and feelings of love quietly returned to my awareness. This all happened within a few minutes while driving only three blocks from where the event occurred.

Depression is another emotion that creates stress and bodily disorder, and it also revolves around hurt. Depression comes when we hold our anger inside and then try to defuse it by attacking ourselves with our own angry thoughts. For this reason, depression involves a double attack on ourselves. First, in response to an external event we attack some aspect of our divine nature such as our love, power, worthiness, or joy, and we feel hurt and then angry comes to protect us from the perceived boundary violation. Next, we turn the anger inward and attack ourselves again with our own thoughts which produces depression. For example, suppose that on her birthday Aunt Tilley does not get an expected present from Cousin Ezra and consequently, feels hurt from the loss of love. It is not the event that produces the hurt; rather it is Aunt Tilley's interpretation of the event, namely, that Cousin Ezra does not love her anymore and that she is therefore not lovable. Unknowingly her attacking thoughts diminish awareness of her own inner love so that she now feels hurt through the loss of love. Angry thoughts then follow in the form of "How dare Cousin Ezra not give me a present after all that I've done for him?" or "He only thinks of himself." When we feel anger produced by such thoughts, we have two choices. We can turn it outward onto the world or inward upon ourselves. When turned inward this anger can translate into such thoughts as "No one has ever loved me" or "I don't deserve presents from others." Turning our anger inward may prevent outbursts against others, but it creates depression within us and feelings of unlovability, powerlessness, or unworthiness. To resolve the depression, we should proceed as when undoing anxiety and anger. We begin by allowing ourselves to feel the depression in our bodies without judging or condemning ourselves for it. Next, we let the depression morph into anger and then we deal with the anger as described above. We then let go of the negative thoughts, our feelings of hurt underlying the anger disappear.

Another technique to undo physical, emotional, and mental holding relationships using a form of the Law of Forgiveness was developed by psychologist Dr. Francine Shapiro, Ph.D. and is called Eye Movement Desensitization and Reprocessing (EMDR). Dr. Shapiro noted that when she moved her eyes from side to side that negative thoughts and emotions that she was experiencing would decrease. Based on her research findings of this experience, she wrote *Eye Movement Desensitization and Reprocessing: Basic Principles, Protocols, and Procedures* in 1995 that detailed the guidelines to treat individuals with various traumas. Recently, it has been used extensively with military individuals diagnosed with PTSD due to their combat service.

Just as the principle of forgiveness or "letting go" is crucial for healthy physical and mental functioning, it is also necessary for proper spiritual functioning. Colin Tipping maintains that we are "spiritual beings having a human experience" and believes that his *Radical Forgiveness* technique can quickly restore our Divine nature. Ironically, our religious views can block us from experiencing the Divine. When they do, we must apply the principle of forgiveness or letting go in the spiritual realm. Doing so connects us with the Imago Deo or the Divine within and thereby puts us in a position to receive the love of God and the fruits of the Holy Spirit. Without forgiveness, we cannot make this connection and can become fixed and rigid, often holding on to religious dogmas and empty rituals.

Buddha warned his followers that blindly accepting dogma and performing mindless rituals could hinder their ability to achieve enlightenment. Jesus continuously criticized the Sadducees and Pharisees in the New Testament for performing meaningless rituals and works without a true connection with the heart of God. "For ye are like whited sepulchers, which indeed appear beautiful outward, Jesus says in Matthew 23: 27, "but within are full of dead bones, and of uncleanness." All of the major religions talk about the need to "let go" of the material world in order to reach the Divine. In Romans 12:2, Christians are advised, "Be not conformed to this world, but be ye transformed by the renewing of your mind," In his book *The Religious Attitude and Life of Islam*, D.B. MacDonald points out that Islamic author Al-Ghazzal maintains that Sufi's, a mystical branch of Islam, focus on separating themselves from everything that is not of God. And finally, Andrew Harvey in *The Essential Mystics* states that Seng Ts'an, the Third Chinese Patriarch of Zen maintains that enlightenment will take one beyond the emptiness of the world.

As in the physical and mental realms of being, the law of forgiveness in the spiritual realm brings healing by letting go of what is blocking our experience of the Divine. The mystic journey according to McColman is a "path of letting go" or detaching ourselves from anything unreal or illusory that blocks our connection to God. Neale Walsch in *Communion with God* also calls us to become aware of the illusions that we have created that separate us from the Divine. By becoming aware of our illusions and letting them go we can remember and connect with our Divine essence.

Which form of forgiveness we use depends upon whether the physical, mental, emotional, or spiritual realms of being are blocking our union with the Divine and need to be undone. There are endless forms of forgiveness that can undo the pain and suffering in this life and facilitate an experience of the Divine. Forgiveness is the one tool that turns us from victims to victors and has no negative side effects. It always points us back to God and does not create any other problems as our other defense coping strategies do. Like the delete button on a computer keyboard, forgiveness releases our holding relationships and frees us to join the "Breath of Life" and we find the place within us where "I know even as I am known" resides. When we are able to let go on each of these levels— physical, mental, emotional, and spiritual— we have undone the holding relationships blocking our awareness of our divine nature and we develop an open heart to God which as we shall see in the next chapter allows our own perfection and God-given powers to surface within us.

# Chapter 4
## THE OPEN HEART

**But rather seek ye the kingdom of God, and all
these things shall be added unto you.**
**Luke 12:31**

Because of free will, we can choose to close our hearts to God and walk away, but it follows that our hardened hearts can only be opened again by us. Unlike the wonderful plant kingdom that always orients itself to the Light, humankind tends to focus away from the Light of God. We are warned in a number of places in the bible to seek God. For example, in Deuteronomy 4:29, we are advised "But if from thence thou shalt seek the Lord thy God, thou shalt find him, if thou seek him with all thy heart and with all thy soul." In Jeremiah 29:13 we are again told, "And ye shall seek me, and find me, when ye shall search for me with all of your heart." Many places in scripture promise that the Divine will respond to our heartfelt calls. In Jeremiah 33:3 God says "Call unto me, and I will answer thee, and show thee great and mighty things, which thou knowest not." In Matthew 7:7-8, Jesus says, "Ask, and it shall be given you; seek, and ye shall find; knock, and it shall be opened unto you; for every one that asketh receiveth; and he that seeketh findeth; and to him that knocketh it shall be open." Likewise, in Luke 11:9, Jesus states, "And I say unto you, ask, and it shall be given you; seek, and ye shall find; knock, and it shall be opened unto you." In Revelation 3:20 Jesus again says "Behold, I stand at the door and knock; if any man hears my voice, and opens the door, I will come in to him, and sup with him, and he with me." These statements show that God and Jesus have great respect for our free will and won't violate the harden heart that we have chosen but will come immediately when we open our hearts and invite them back.

In Matthew 6:33, Jesus says "But seek ye first the kingdom of God and his righteousness, And all these things shall be added unto you." So, what are the things that will be added to us when we let go of our hardened hearts and have an open heart to God? According to Proverbs 2:6 "For the Lord giveth wisdom; out of his mouth cometh knowledge and understanding and again in Ecclesiastes 2:26 "For God giveth to a man that is good in his sight wisdom, and knowledge, and joy." Psalms 84:11 says "For the Lord is a sun and shield; The Lord will give grace and glory: no good thing will be withheld from them that walk uprightly." Jeremiah 31:33 declares "I will put my law in their inward parts, and write it in their hearts, and will be their God, and they shall be my people." Mark 9:23 says "All things are possible to him that believeth." 2 Peter 1:3 says that "According as his divine power hath given unto us all things that pertain to life and godliness, through the knowledge of him that hath called us to glory and virtue while 2 Peter 1:4 states, "Whereby are given unto us exceeding great and precious promises that by these ye might be partakers of the divine nature having escaped the corruption that is in the world through lust."

When we open our hearts to God, we are told in Psalm 36:9 that we connect with the "fountain of life" itself: "For with thee is the fountain of life; in thy light shall we see light." This "fountain of life" can be likened to the Zero Point Energy field discussed in quantum physics. In his book *Quantum Physics for Beginners: Quantum Mechanics and Quantum Theory Explained*, Jason Stephenson points out that classical physics, based on Newtonian theory, is very deterministic and defines the rules for how big, visible things in our universe behave while quantum theory is uncertain and random; thus, it explains the rules for how little invisible things behave in terms of probabilities. By way of example, consider the quantum Law of Entanglement which states that electrons distantly located from each other can be linked and share information instantly. However, on a macro scale where classical physics operates all things are bound by the speed of light and the Law of Entanglement does not apply.

Gregg Braden, in *The Divine Matrix,* suggests that the Law of Entanglement explains why twins who are separate and have no communication with one another often act as if they are still together. He concluded from these observations and other scientific experiments that everything exists within a field he called the Divine Matrix. It is highly likely that the Law of Entanglement also explains what psychoanalysis Dr. Carl G. Jung, MD called synchronicity or situations when we think of someone and out of the blue they appear or call us. All things are considered to be connected within the Divine Matrix, which is also holographic and thus contains the past, present, and future in every part. Lynne McTaggart, in *The Field,* points out that quantum physicists call this strange law in the subatomic world "nonlocality" and said that Einstein referred to it as "spooky action at a distance." She reviewed the work of many well known physicists and scientific researchers who agreed there was no such thing as a vacuum of nothingness or emptiness in space rather space is full of subatomic particles going in and out of existence. This reservoir in space has been called the Zero Point Energy Field because it reflects fluctuations of energy at temperatures of absolute zero where all matter has been removed and nothing is left to make any motion. The behavior of quantum particles in the zero energy field is like a ball in a tennis match in that energy in the form of photons, electrons, and other quantum particles are continually passed back and forth in and out of existence and this movement creates tremendous energy. It is here that the Newtonian idea of cause and effect does not apply rather one can predict events only by using probability theory.

Whether we use the term the Divine Matrix or the Zero Point Energy Field, it seems reasonable to conclude that these two concepts could be what Psalm 36:9 calls "the fountain of life." Since this energy field is considered to be a hologram and thus contains all information including the past, present, and future in every part, if we connect with it, we can have a pipeline to all knowledge just as Proverbs 2:6 and

Ecclesiastes 2:26 states in the bible. According to Heinz R. Pagels in *The Cosmic Code: Quantum Physics as the Language of Nature,* Einstein "seemed to have a hotline to the 'Old One' which was Einstein's term for God." In Jeremiah 33:3, God says "Call unto me, and I will answer thee, and show thee great and mighty things, which thou knowest not" which indicates that everyone has been created with the potential to connect with God and thus receive the "fountain of life" as stated in Psalm 36.9 "For with thee (God) is the fountain of life: in thy light we shall see light." The ability to connect with God or the zero energy field provides a good explanation for how biblical prophets were able to see into the future.

Another law in quantum theory maintains that humans can influence the structure of the physical world. This law says that an event in the subatomic world is random or exists in all possible states until a human observer attends and measures some part of it and this reduces it to a single state. Is this what happens with prayers, decrees, and affirmations made by humankind? In her book *The Field,* Lynne McTaggart reviewed the work of physicist Dr. Hal Puthoff who thought that the zero energy field might possibly be manipulated by humankind to provide energy for operating cars and space travel as well as providing explanations for many metaphysical events observed by humankind. Dr. Puthoff wondered if levitation, the ability to move objects by focusing one's attention on them, could be explained by the zero energy field concept. McTaggart concluded from Dr. Puthoff's work that this field could explain how the techniques of homeopathy, acupuncture, and remote spiritual healing could affect others instantaneously. Since the field is the connection between everything including humankind then it follows that information in the form of thoughts can affect the structure of the physical world and instantaneously be transmitted to someone else. This could explain how God, Jesus, and the Holy Spirit can hear our prayers and instantly respond to us with help."

Further evidence lending credence to the idea that humankind can affect the physical world can be seen in the research work of physicist Dr. Helmut Schmidt. Dr. Schmidt developed a random number generator (RNG) machine with four colored lights (red, yellow, green, and blue) on top which would flash on randomly. He used subjects who possessed psychic gifts and found that they could produce successful results that were higher than the results probability predicted. However, this test did not provide information on whether the results were due to precognition (seeing into the future) or psychokinesis (the ability to move objects in space). Dr. Schmidt then proceeded to develop another machine to measure psychokinesis. His new machine was the electronic version of flipping a coin used by parapsychologist Dr. J.B. Rhine in his dice studies. This machine generated random sequences of heads and tails that were displayed by the movement of a light in a circle of nine lamps. Dr. Schmidt designed a research protocol in which his psychically gifted subjects were asked to will the lights to take steps in a clockwise direction and thus produce more heads than tails. Across a series of studies, he found a significant effect with people who had psychic gifts but their scores indicated that their intentions produced reversed effects on the machine. That is, if they willed the lights to go in a clockwise direction and produce more heads than tails, the machine went in a counterclockwise direction and more tails were produced. Based on his studies, Dr. Schmidt concluded that human will was affecting the RNG machine and statically this was a major effect with a probability of a thousand to one that the result occurred by chance alone.

Dr. Robert Jahn, Ph.D., an engineering professor, then developed the Random Event Generator (REG) to control for any hardware device failures that could cause deviations from the normal 50-50 chance of a heads and tails probability sequence found in the Rhine and Schmidt studies. Dr. Jahn also refined the scientific protocols used in past studies including the use of ordinary people rather than psychically gifted people in his experiments. He found that these subjects were able to affect the random movement of the REG machine by "an act of will."

These studies provide scientific evidence that humankind has the ability to produce changes in the physical world but how is this accomplished? In a dictation dated January 23, 1949 Guy W. Ballard, Founder of the Saint Germain I AM Foundation, stated that when we anchored our attention and life energy onto the outer physical world and away from God or our inner I AM Presence, this focus not only creates all of our problems in life but blocks us from our true abilities to precipitate miracles and command and control nature. It follows from this that we need to open our hearts and maintain our connection with the Divine. In Luke 12: 31, Jesus says, "Seek ye the kingdom of God: and all these things shall be added unto you." So, when we connect with the image of God within us, we are connecting with the zero-energy field or the "fountain of life." Therefore, we receive all wisdom, all knowledge, and "all things that pertain to life." We recover our powers to produce miracles in the world and to command and control nature like Moses, Elijah, Elisha, Saint Paul, and Jesus."

In her *Law of Life Book I,* A. D. K. Luk points out that humankind has three basic powers including attention, vision, and feeling that can be used to precipitate changes in the physical world. She explained that we have been endowed by God with these creative abilities, which are the root activities for controlling, producing, and manifesting changes in the external world. First, we have to open ourselves to connect with God or the zero energy field and then direct our attention to a thing in the external world that we want to change or to the vision of the thing that we want to manifest. When we attend to something, we are directing Life energy to go there. We are compelling energy from the I AM Presence or the Divine to flow there and in this way what our attention is focused on can be changed or we can out picture something new into the world. This is why it is very important not to focus on the negative because you open the door for it to come into you.

To obtain what you want to manifest, you also have to feel the pleasure of already having what you want or are visualizing. In Christian biblical teachings, the New Testament describes how we can command nature and make changes in the world. Matthew 17:19 reports "Then came the disciples to Jesus apart, and said, why could not we cast him out?" and in Matthew 17:20 Jesus said "Because of your unbelief; for verily I say unto you, if ye have faith as a grain of mustard seed, ye shall say unto this mountain, remove from here to yonder place; and it shall remove; and nothing shall be impossible unto you." Here Jesus is saying that we have to have faith in order for our prays, decrees, and commands to be manifested.

In Hebrews 11:1, faith is defined as the substance of things hoped for, the evidence of things not seen. This definition involves doing two things to command and control nature or precipitate something from the "fountain of life" or the zero-energy field. First, we need to have a very clear tangible vision or image of the thing or event that we want to happen in our minds and then feel hope that it will appear. The Hebrew word for hope is "elpizo," which according to Zodhiates, Spiros Zodhiates, Th. D. and Warren Baker, D.R.E. (Editors) of *Hebrew-Greek Keyword Study Bible KJV* means to expect or anticipate with pleasure and confidence. Therefore, it follows that in order to produce miracles and command nature, we need to hold a clear image of what we want and then call it forth with the emotion of confidence and also, according to G. W. Ballard, actually feel the pleasure from experiencing that this has happen before it has happened in the external world. Many people see pray as begging God to give us something that we believe we do not deserve. In the 1930s, the I AM teachings including the Saint Germain Foundation of G. W. Ballard and the Unity Church founded by Charles Filmore emphasized using decrees and affirmations to affect changes in the world rather than pleading to God for things. This approach seems to match Jesus' behavior when he quietened the storm by commanding it to be still and when he said to the fig tree "Let no fruit grow on thee henceforth forever" and it withered away and died (Matthew 21:19). In Matthew 21:21-22, Jesus then said "Verily I say unto you, If ye have faith and doubt not... Ye shall not only do this which is done to the fig tree, but also if ye shall say unto this mountain, Be thou removed, and be thou cast into the sea; it shall be done and all things, whatsoever ye shall ask in pray believing ye shall receive." Clearly from these statements, Jesus is directing us to use decrees, affirmations, or commands to effect changes in the world.

As stated in the last chapter, we create an open heart by applying the Law of Forgiveness and letting go of the holding relationships in our hardened hearts which then allows us to connect with God and the "fountain of life" or the Zero Point Energy field discussed in quantum theory. The Law of Forgiveness also allows us to achieve and maintain our connection with the Divine or Zero Energy Field and thus our ability to control and create things in the outer world. At this point, I began to wonder if the Law of Forgiveness that is so vital an activity in our spiritual growth and connection with the Divine could be explained in quantum theory terms. With this idea in my mind, I began to search for such a law in quantum theory. It was not long before I came across the Law of Entropy, which is the second law of thermodynamics. Entropy is defined as the amount of energy that is not available for work during a certain process or closed system and relates to its internal state of disorder— high entropy levels are disordered states and low entropy levels are characteristic of ordered states. A system is closed when no energy is being added to or removed from it. Energy becomes unavailable, not by leaving the system, but by becoming irretrievably disordered as a consequence of the laws of statistical mechanics. In *The Human Use of Human Beings*, mathematician Dr. Nobert Wiener, Ph.D. stated that all closed systems in the universe tend to deteriorate and return to the chaotic or disordered state observed in the zero-energy field. He further states that humans are not closed systems as they can take in food and supply themselves with energy and thereby restore their vitality.

When we use the Law of Forgiveness to release our holding relationships, we are directing our minds to let go of or disperse the thoughts, senses, and emotions forming these relationships. The thoughts, emotions, senses, and perceptions that form our holding relationships are all bottom line just energy—that is, atoms or protons, neutrons, and electrons bound together. Since the Law of Entropy describes the activity of releasing ordered energy back into the movement of protons, electrons and neutrons in a type of nonordered random state, it acts like the activity of the Law of Forgiveness, which we have the ability to use to release, disperse, or let go of our negative holding relationships. In Hebrews 11:1, faith is defined as the substance of things hoped for, the evidence of things not seen. Humans have a tendency to hold on to hurts, disappointments, slights, and other lack of expressions of love, which produce hardened hearts, thereby blocking our connection with God and our God given powers. It is interesting to note that holding onto the hurts and slights from others is more difficult in the sense that it requires a lot more energy to hold and maintain them than to let them go and permit the natural flow of the Law of Entropy to disperse these painful events, thereby allowing their subatomic components to return to a state of disorder and randomness in the zero-energy field. When we are unforgiving, we are going against the nature flow of life.

In everyday life, we all experience the fact that our universe tends toward disorder. Parents are very aware of this when they walk into a child's room and discover toys dispersed everywhere in the room. We can also see this tendency toward disorder in such commonly used modern inventions as a car and a house both of which start falling apart a few years after they are constructed. No matter what the complex invention, the invention itself will never maintain its complex order without some type of intelligent help. For example, with use of their intelligent minds, the room can be ordered again either by the parents or by their directions to the child to pick up the toys. Likewise, the car and house can be restored by the intervention of an adult's intelligent mind that reduces the disorder brought on by entropy by hiring a professional or doing the repair alone. This fact argues for an Intelligent Creator having created the universe just as we here in the physical world order our own universes. In metaphysical teachings this would follow from the Law of Correspondence—as above, so below. In the Lord's prayer (Matthew 6:9-13 and Luke 11:1-4), we call for "Thy kingdom come, Thy will be done in earth, as it is in heaven which is a command for what is above to be below."

Although many people have experienced an open heart for the Divine and connection with their Divine powers, it is typically very difficult for most people to maintain such mountain top experiences in their daily life. Clues as to how to maintain a connection with the Divine or Zero Point Energy field can be found in a dictation dated January 23, 1949 by Guy W. Ballard, Founder of the Saint Germain I AM Foundation. Mr. Ballard stated that we need to anchor our attention and therefore our life energy onto God or our inner I AM Presence. Traditional Christian scripture also emphasizes that we need to keep our focus on God. In Hebrews 11: 24-26, we are told that Moses stayed focused on God and valued this relationship above all the riches of Egypt. Moses esteemed his God given mission above everything.

In *Keys to Staying Full of God*, Andrew Wommack delineates four keys to maintaining a connection with God based on Romans 1:21: "Because that, when they knew God, they glorified him not as God, neither were thankful; but became vain in their imaginations, and their foolish heart was darkened." The Greek word for glorify is "doxazo" which according to the *Hebrew-Greek Keyword Study Bible KJV* means to render, esteem, honor, magnify, or to give praise and adoration. The Greek word for thankful is "eucharisteo" which means to be thankful or grateful while the word for "became vain" is "mataioo" which means to render foolish, wicked, or worthless. The Greek word for heart is "kardia" and refers the seat of the intellect meaning the mind or understanding. Based on these Greek meanings of the words in Romans 1:21, it is easy to see how Wommack concluded that to remain connected to God we need to do four things: glorify God, be thankful or grateful to God, recognize the power of our imaginations, and have a good heart.

So how do we apply these steps in our everyday lives? When we find ourselves in a bad situation, we need to use our ability to focus or attend with our ability to visualize or imagine with our mind's eye to look away from the negative situation or problem and focus on God and the mission that God gave us to complete. Once we have this clearly in our minds, we glorify God by bringing forth the emotions of praise, honor, esteem, and adoration and let them flow to God. It is also important at this point to be thankful and express this gratitude to God. A state of being grateful opens our heart to love and when we radiate this to God, we close a circuit and will receive a loving radiation back from God. In Hebrews 12: 2, we see how Jesus "endured the cross, despising the shame." "Despising the shame" according to Andrew Wommack in *Keys to Staying Full of God* suggested that Jesus focused His attention away from the negative part of the crucifixion and placed it on God and His mission. This can also be thought of as an application of faith as described in Hebrews 11:1 where faith is defined as the substance of things hoped for, the evidence of things not seen. Here, Jesus focuses on God and accomplishing His divine mission on earth instead of the pain and suffering of the crucifixion."

In *HeartMath Solutions* published in 1999, Doc Childe, Howard Martin, and Donna Beech provide scientific evidence confirming that many of the spiritual suggestions from the Bible as to how to create an open and loving heart were in fact correct. These authors went beyond the current paradigm of seeing the brain as the master organ of the body with the heart serving only a physical blood pumping function within the body. Their research indicated that the heart not the brain was the master organ of the body. This is not an entirely new idea since the Greek word for heart is "kardia" and refers the seat of the intellect meaning the mind or understanding. Their work has brought the idea of following your heart from the realm of literature, religion, and philosophy into the realm of scientific investigation that has resulted in new information about heart intelligence along with the introduction of new techniques and exercises to acquire a harmonious, intelligent heart. These authors reported scientific findings that the heart has "its own brain" consisting of about 40,000 neurons and many neural axons that travel to the brain. There are neurons in the limbic system of the brain often called the reptilian brain that are sensitive to the activity in the heart. They concluded that heart intelligence was like emotional intelligence and observed that positive emotions produced order and balance in the autonomic nervous system (a state of coherence) while negative emotions caused the nervous system to be out of balance with "jagged and disordered heart rhythms" and an increased production of the stress hormone cortisol (a state of incoherence). Their subjects also reported that when their heart rhythms were balanced and harmonious, they experienced "increased mental clarity and intuition." Their research indicates that the brain was the seat of linear, logical intelligence while heart intelligence is "intuitive and a type of direct knowing" that expands our overall intellectual range."

In *Heartmath Solutions*, exercises are presented to help achieve a harmonious heart. They involve the use of such "core heart feelings" as love, compassion, nonjudgment, courage, forgiveness, appreciation, gratitude, and care, which produce harmonious heart rhythms. The core heart feelings to harmonize the heart are very similar to what Romans 1:21 directs us to do to connect with God. We are told to glorify God and develop a sense gratefulness to God. By doing this we open our hearts and connect with God or the zero-energy field and can maintain a connection to the Divine for extended periods of time. The next chapter will discuss the stages we go through in opening ourselves to the Divine and beyond.

# *Chapter 5*
## THE EXPERIENCE

**And the Lord God formed man of the dust of
the ground, and breathed into his nostrils the
breath of life; and man became a living soul.**
**Genesis 2:7**

When we let go of our holding relationships with the external world of people, things, and actions, the Divine within returns into our consciousness like the morning sun rising in the eastern sky. We reconnect with what Chief Luther Standing Bear of the Teton Sioux tribe calls the unifying force that was breathed into us and into all things by Wakan Tanka, The Great Spirit. This connection is our door into eternity — into the zero-energy field. It is the place where we greet God and God greets us—where we know as we are known. As Bebe Griffiths in *Return to the Center* says our consciousness contains a window in which we can look into Eternity and where Eternity can look out into the world of space and time. He states that it is here that we discover our real Self. Clearly, Griffiths has found the door to eternity or the Zero Energy field within himself.

Jesus too promises that we can find an eternal reality–a kingdom within us. Although the Gnostic gospels of the Dead Sea Scrolls emphasize an immanent God within who can be known, the canonical gospels in the King James Version of the Bible generally view God more as a transcendent being who is mostly unknowable. Black Elk, an

Oglala Sioux medicine man, spiritual leader, and author also believed that there is a space within our hearts where Great Spirit dwells, thus, enabling us to see all things. At this place, "the Eye of the Great Spirit" or the "Kingdom within," we can join the "breath of life" and surf the Great River of Life or the zero energy field. We can see forever!

In this chapter, I will discuss the six stages that I have found to be consistently associated with moving through this veil to the Divine or into the Zero-Energy field. Since my purpose is to help others learn how to reconnect with the Divine within or zero energy field and maintain this connection, I will concentrate more on an experiential rather than on an academic or theoretical description of the experience. I will describe each stage of this process with my own personal experiences as well as the experiences of people from many different religious faiths.

Before discussing what I do to initiate this mystical experience and define the six stages of such an experience, I should point out that some mystics—among them Robert May in *Cosmic Consciousness Revisited*—maintain that mystical experiences happen by the grace of God and not by our doing. Carl McColman similarly stresses in *The Aspiring Mystic*, that a mystical experience involves two parties: you and the object of your attention. He stresses that just wanting to unite with the Divine and open ourselves to such experiences does not guarantee that we will have them. Nevertheless, within Christianity, we are also told, "Draw nigh to God and he will draw nigh unto you" (James 4:8) and to "knock, and it shall be opened unto you" (Luke 11: 9). This seems to suggest that we first begin with a willingness or desire to encounter the Divine and then to approach Him. Only by setting the stage for a mystical experience can we hope that the Divine will smile on us and reveal His heart. We "draw nigh" by opening ourselves to God through some application of the principle or Law of Forgiveness.

Although forgiveness is our primary tool, we can also use what Marghanita Laski called "triggers" to initiate mystical experiences. Triggers are events that help us let go of the thin veil that seems to separate us from the Divine. Laski studied a number of transcendental experiences and in her book, *Ecstasy*, identified nature, architecture (particularly that of churches), poetry, music, and sexual love as important triggers for eliciting them. In *The Spiritual Nature of Man*, Sir Alister Hardy concluded that meditation, prayer, natural beauty, sacred places, the arts, literature, sex, and personal relationships could also serve as triggers. R.A. Gilbert concluded that between both "Laski and Hardy the whole of human experience can be considered a fruitful source of potential stimuli for attaining transcendental states of consciousness." Eckhart Tolle in *The Power of the Now* also argues that anything can become a portal through which the "unmanifested" can manifest itself. "Grief, suffering, fear, or rage may all be doorways into the infinite," McColman adds, "as surely as love, joy, and peace may be."

Huston Smith in *World Religions* points out that Hindus, believing in many paths to the Divine, recommend approaching it through whatever type of yoga is best suited to our personality. Jnana yoga is considered best for people who are reflective. This form of yoga, according to Smith, is "an intuitive discernment that transforms, turning the knower eventually into that which is known" Bhakti yoga is the most popular form and is considered best for those who are emotional. It uses devotion, love, and adoration for the Divine as a way to achieve union. Karma yoga is prescribed for people of action and involves doing good works as a way to transcend the ego and connect with the Divine. Raja yoga is considered the best path for people who are scientific and involves doing mental exercises and observing their effects.

Huston Smith believes that when Carl Jung posited personality types based on thinking, intuiting, feeling, sensing, perceiving, and judging he borrowed the basic idea from Hindu religious thinking. Jung believed that these functions, with some dominant and others inferior, comprised our individual personalities. Accordingly, he maintains that when we assimilate our inferior functions in a balanced relationship with our opposite, superior functions, we achieve a sense of wholeness. For example, if a person were dominant in intuition, then sensing would be the inferior or less developed of this pair of functions, and to experience wholeness and personality integration, the person would have to assimilate the sensing function in a balanced relationship with the more superior intuitive function. I have often wondered if people of a mystical bent are naturally more intuitive and that is why going into the sensory world of nature has been such a common path by which they have achieved mystical experiences.

Although every person seeking an experience with the Divine needs to discover what works best for him or her, I have had practically all of my experiences in nature. In this, I am not unusual. As William James in *Varieties of Religious Experience* notes, most mystical experiences occur in nature. Jesus went into the wilderness for forty days and Moses went to the top of a mountain to receive revelations. Buddha received enlightment while sitting under the Bodhi tree after a long retreat into the forest of his homeland. Muhammad is reported to have retreated to a cave on the outskirts of Mecca, where he realized, "There is no god but God" and received his appointment to do God's work. He rushed home to tell his wife that he was either a prophet or a madman.

In *The Wisdom of the Native American*, Kent Newburn notes that Native Americans, in general, view nature as a temple and the worship of the Great Mystery to be silent and solitary. "We would deem it sacrilege to build a house," he says, "for The One who may be met face to face in the mysterious, shadowy aisles of the primeval forest." Similarly, Buddha saw no need for a church institution or a group of priests to help us reach the state that he called enlightenment. His last words were reported to be, "Work out your own salvation with diligence...be a lamp unto yourself." These words resonate with me, for although I was reared in the Christian tradition, I practice my faith more in the vein of Buddha and the Native Americans. As it was for my Cherokee great grandmother, nature is my church and where I have had most of my experiences of the Divine. My worship is also silent and solitary and my prayers are to recognize the "Unseen" rather than to petition for the seen. "Silence is to the mystic," wrote McColman, "what soil is to the tulip.

In Psalm 46:10, David wrote, "Be still and know that I am God." To find such silence, I retreat from the work-a-day world and begin a session to connect with the Divine by planning a trip into nature. I personally like situations near the water with open, windy skies. In the first three stages of this experience, open spaces help me to become aware and to feel myself as a small, finite observer of an infinitely larger nature. In the Kinesthetic-Cognitive stage they lead me away from feeling separated or in a part-to-whole relationship with nature to feeling at one with nature. In the later stages of a mystical experience, this part-to-whole relationship that I experience with nature in open spaces is translated into a type of I-Thou relationship with the Divine that transcends the natural world of appearances.

Eckhart Tolle believes like me that the Divine (or what he calls the "Unmanifested") can be found in silence and open spaces. He believes that paying attention to the space around us instead of to the objects contained in the space causes an inner shift in our consciousness. He suggests that thoughts, emotions, and sense impressions are objects in our minds much as furniture, trees, and hills are objects in space outside of ourselves. By focusing on external space, we can shift our internal awareness away from mind objects to the space of "no-mind" or the empty, quiet mind spoken of the eastern religions. But we are still using the principle of forgiveness because we are letting go of our attachments to objects and focusing on space. In this way space can become a portal to an experience of the Divine or zero-energy Field.

I also find that wind is very helpful in moving me through the stages of this experience. It stimulates the sense of touch when it blows across my skin. It caresses the body, gently beckoning it to let go and join with nature in the first stages of the experience and then with the universe and the Divine in the later stages. I think that we must each experiment to learn which elements of nature— wind, fire, water, textures, sights, sounds, time of day—are the most effective in undoing our holding relationships and emptying our minds of negative thoughts and our bodies of stressful emotions and sensations. Be aware that if a particular element that you ordinarily use is absent, it may prevent the experience. For example, I have found that in the absence of wind, I begin a session more aware of my inner feelings and with a stronger sense of separation from nature. This change is important only in that it determines where I begin to let go and thus what form of forgiveness I use to do it. When there is no wind, I begin letting go of my feelings with the Cognitive-Feeling techniques introduced in Chapter 3. I also focus on other elements in nature by shifting my attention to its vibrant colors and many shapes that help me enter the first stages of experiencing the Divine.

In teaching people how to have a mystical experience, I have found to my surprise that many of them feel frightened and very vulnerable in nature. I never had such feelings, since my father, who loved nature, taught me to love it as a very young child. I can still remember sitting with him on our front porch, watching lightning flashes leaping around storm clouds and feeling safe and secure. But for people who do have negative holding relationships with nature, the first step in having a mystical experience must be either to undo this reaction to nature or to find an alternative setting.

Sharon Burch, a Navajo musician and singer, created a wonderful CD called "Colors of my Heart", in which, like a mother comforting a child, she sings about the forces of nature. Listening to her songs may help undo negative holding relationships with nature. A number of other relaxation and desensitization techniques can also be used to facilitate the letting go process. The task begins with becoming consciously aware of the thinking that produces these negative feelings toward nature and ends with releasing them. Another difficulty I have found is that some people are afraid to be by themselves. Unlike many Native Americans, they are afraid "to be silent and to be solitary." Although the reasons for their fears are varied, solutions to it are available. Personally, I like to be alone and in fact feel more energized and connected to everything when alone. Through trial and error, I have learned to plan my trips into nature well so that being hungry or too full, or too thirsty or tired or too hot or cold will not keep my focus on my bodily sensations and interfere with having an experience of the Divine. I prefer to remain on the hungry side, since this creates an inner sense of aliveness and innervation that in turn promotes a desire for activity and moving around in the world.

I have also found music helpful in initiating religious experiences. The form, as well as the content of the music we choose should create a sense of expansiveness and be uplifting to both body and spirit. It should bring us to focus in the here-and-now or present moment, facilitate a sense of bodily well-being, and increase a sense of flowing in our minds. During the early part of the experience, the degree to which the music creates a sense of expansion is particularly important since it helps us to disconnect from the objects in space and to focus on space itself.

If the form or instrumental aspect of the music also creates good harmony in our body, we can more easily walk through the first three stages of a mystical experience, better experiencing the flow of the sensory world in the Cognitive-Emptying stage and the order and unity of nature in the Sensory-Synchronizing stage. Music can also help us blend our kinesthetic sense with our other senses and with nature in the Kinesthetic-Cognitive stage. The content of the music that we select refers to the meaning communicated by the words in the music. It should create an uplifting of our spirit and mind in order to help us walk through the remaining stages of connecting with the Divine.

My choices in music over the last 10 years have varied. I began by listening to Beverly Hutchinson's readings from *A Course in Miracles* that used Steve Halpern's music as background. Her works include "The Ark of Peace," "The Holy Instant," "You are Entitled to Miracles," "The Forgotten Song," and many others. In recent years, I have turned to instrumentals and chants from such Native American artists as Douglas Spotted Eagle, David and Steve Gordon, and Joanne Shenandoah. I am almost guaranteed a full-blown mystical experience when I listen to Spotted Eagle's "Closer to Far Away." The first and second "Sacred Spirits" CDs are also helpful in producing experiences of the Divine. Over the years, I have found that music, which once was of great help eventually fades in its ability to trigger a mystical experience. Again, some people find that other types of music or no music at all works best to induce a mystical experience. McColman reported that such classical works as Beethoven's Ninth Symphony and Bach's Toccata and Fugue in D Minor worked for him. We must each discover the music that serves us best in our spiritual journey to the Divine.

Descriptions of mystical experiences have ranged from very broad ones like that of Neale Donald Walsch in *Communion with God* to those that only detail sudden experiences of the Divine as in the writings of William James, Dr. Richard Burke, and Robert May. "First we become aware of that which is Divine around us," writes Walsch, before we become aware of "that which is Divine within us." And then, "We become aware all is Divine and that there is nothing else." James, Burke, and May describe in detail the flow of awareness in sudden mystical experiences as arising first from the outside then progressing to an experience of the Divine within us. Based on my experiences, I have discerned six distinct stages in a mystical experience or the passage "through the door to eternal life" where "I know as I am known." They include the Cognitive-Emptying Stage, the Sensory-Synchronizing Stage, the Kinesthetic-Cognitive Stage, the Being stage, the Receiving Stage, and the Extending Stage. Each stage of the experience is achieved by applying some form of the Law of Forgiveness or "letting go." When we let go of our holding relationships with the world, we undo the blocks reinforcing our separation from the Divine. If we let go of more and more of this separation, we will re-unite with the Divine and experience deeper and deeper levels of our inner love for the Divine in us. As we experience more of our inner love, our desire to unite with the universe and ultimately with the Divine in us also grows. Our desire for separation is dispelled in favor of one for joining. In this way our inner love and desire to unite propels us forward through the various stages of connection with the Divine.

I will present these stages in the order in which they seem to consistently occur in my experience. In reality, I encountered bits and pieces of the stages of this process at different times in my life. Only through the luxury of looking back across forty years of such experiences was I able to see how they fit together. I also realize now that the aspect of the connection that I experienced depended upon my psychological needs at the time. For example, when I needed harmony and order to heal my inner discord, I pursued and lingered in the Sensory-Synchronizing stage. During the early 1970s when I was trying to discover my self-identity, I spent most of my time seeking and experiencing the Being stage. When I needed to heal some emotional hurt I often sought the Receiving stage, where Divine love was waiting to heal me. After opening my private practice in the late 1980s, I concentrated mainly on the Receiving stage, so that I would be filled with love, which I could then extend to my patients during their therapy. By extending love back into the world we become more and more aware of our true inner power. While writing this book, I opened myself to cycling through all six stages of this process, stopping in a particular stage only to observe and record my experiences there.

Like cell division on the biological level, a mystical experience is a process of change and its stages are not rigidly fixed. Each one involves a number of characteristics that can be experienced in varying degrees of intensity in any one session, and perhaps not at all in another session. We may occasionally spend more time in one stage than in another or experience one stage to the exclusion of all the others. In *Cosmic Consciousness Revisited*, Robert May concluded that as Dante suggested in the *Divine Comedy*, our inner journey can be both slow and spontaneous. He believed that we could slowly travel through hell and then experience a seemingly sudden transport to paradise. We can also, without warning, be swept into a stage of the process where we have an intense experience of the Divine.

Dr. Bucke, in *Cosmic Consciousness*, concluded that the "suddenness of the awakening" was the crucial characteristic of a real encounter with the Divine or of what he termed an experience of "cosmic consciousness." His label of some experiences as "lesser, imperfect, and doubtful" instances seems to be references to what I am calling different stages in the mystical experience. Saint Paul's conversion on the road to Damascus is a commonly known example of such an intense and unexpected experience of God. Dr. Bucke noted that many people have had these sudden experiences of the Divine, including Dante, Boehme, St. John of the Cross, Walt Whitman, and Henry David Thoreau. In *Varieties of Religious Experience*, William James also reported many sudden experiences of God. He cites J. Trevor, who in his autobiography *My Quest for God* writes of such an experience while walking along a road. "Suddenly, without warning," he wrote, "I felt that I was in Heaven—an inward state of peace and joy and assurance indescribably intense, accompanied with a sense of being bathed in a warm glow of light, as though the external condition had brought about the internal effect—a feeling of having passed beyond the body, though the scene around stood out more clearly and as if nearer to me than before, by reason of the illumination in the midst of which I seemed to be placed. This deep emotion lasted, though with decreasing strength, until I reached home and for some time after only gradually passing away."

The first stage of a mystical experience is what I call the Cognitive-Emptying Stage because it involves "letting go," or "emptying" our minds of all reflections on the past and all thoughts of the future as well as those thoughts that produce negative feelings or stressful bodily sensations. When we empty our minds of all thoughts, positive as well as negative, we undo the blocks hiding the Divine within from our awareness. "We have to surrender to the now," writes Tolle, "before we can connect with the Unmanifested that lies beyond our cluttering mind and shifting emotions." This stage results at first in a quiet, undistracted mind, and a sense of the "Void" or the "Great Emptiness," but ends with a feeling of love and a desire to join with everything.

Many religions stress the importance of the Cognitive-Emptying stage as a prerequisite for re-uniting with the Divine. Swami A.C. Bhaktivedanta in *The Bhagavad Gita as It Is* discusses the importance in Hinduism of undoing our material entanglements in order to live in "union with a Cosmic player." He writes that "a person who is not disturbed by the incessant flow of desires—that enter like rivers into the ocean which is ever being filled but is always still—can alone achieve peace: and not the man who strives to satisfy such desires. A person who has given up all desires for sense gratification, who lives free from desires, who has given up all sense of proprietorship, and is devoid of false ego—he alone can attain real peace. That is the way of the spiritual and godly life, after attaining which a man is not bewildered, being so situated, even at the house of death, one can enter into the Kingdom of God.

William Barrett in *Zen Buddhism* noted that Zen is "a philosophy to undo philosophy," and that its methods focus on stripping us of our thoughts so that we can enter the "Great Emptiness." If we remain in this emptiness "and do not run away in fear, this great void may bloom with all manner of miracles, and heaven and earth, in consort once again, engender effortlessly all their ancient marvels." W.Y. Evans-Wentz in *The Tibetan Book of the Dead* said that realization of the Void is the main purpose and, in this Void, lies the essence of the universe and essential wisdom [Bodhi]. Buddha, using the one-pointed concentration form of meditation to let go of the ego and of all desire for the material world attained a state of nonattachment, or Nirvana—a super worldly state of Being. Kent Newburn in *The Wisdom of the Native American* points out that in general Native Americans believe that each soul must meet the morning sun, the new sweet earth, and the Great Silence alone." For Native Americans, silence is the balance of body, mind, and spirit.

In *The Power of the Now*, Eckhart Tolle speaks of listening for the silence from which sounds arise. "Paying attention to outer silence," he says, "creates inner silence and the mind becomes still." In this inner silence, a portal opens and through it we can feel the presence of the Divine. The teachings of Jesus also emphasize letting go of material entrapments of the world in favor of the treasures of heaven. "Love not the world, neither the things of the world", He says in I John 2:15. So it is clear that although Christianity, Hinduism, Buddhism, Zen Buddhism, and Native American religions differ in form, terminology, and techniques, they are all alike in maintaining that we need to let go of things in the world to unite with the Divine. Their seemingly different techniques to achieving this union are also alike in that they are all based on applying the Law of Forgiveness or "letting go" to achieve the "Void," the "Great Emptiness," or the "Great Silence."

The type of forgiveness that we use to achieve the Cognitive-Emptying stage of this experience depends on the type of holding relationships that we need to undo. If stress-derived bodily sensations are blocking our ability to join the Divine, we may need to use several of the techniques discussed in Chapter 3. We may need to use the somatic free association technique, basic relaxation procedures, the Alexander technique, EMDR, or some combination of these to identify and empty ourselves of stress, strain, or disorder in our bodies. Just as we need to clear our bodies of distracting sensations, we may also need to let go of such negative emotions as anxiety, anger, and depression. Here, we can use the cognitive-feeling techniques discussed earlier to undo such feelings serving to block experiences of the Divine. We can begin by accepting and then identifying our negative feelings before moving to the cognitive level to determine the thoughts that are producing them. Once we have identified the thinking, we can correct it and therefore release the feelings. Then, having emptied ourselves of bodily sensations and of emotions, we must empty our minds of thoughts as well. The Western mind is typically a beehive of racing and buzzing thoughts, and to let its activity go can be both difficult and frightening. But to this end, we can use the thought-stopping technique described earlier to empty our minds of such thoughts. If something is troubling us deeply, it may be necessary to apply this technique more than once, but with practice we can do it almost effortlessly.

Once we have emptied ourselves of our thoughts and of our emotional and bodily reactions to them, we experience calmness and being in the sensory world in the here-and-now. By our sensory world, I mean the experiences that our senses provide us— the smells, sights, sounds, tastes, and textures that surround us. The here-and-now aspect of this experience points to the feeling that time involves only the present. We experience ourselves as existing in the present sensory moment, undistracted by thoughts of the past or future. In everyday life, we experience time as a linear progression extending from the past to the future. But in eternity everything exists simultaneously and there is no progression of time. When we enter the here-and-now experience, we have taken our first steps toward an awareness of eternity where time has no segments. Walt Whitman's "Song of Myself" shows the poet enraptured in this first stage of a mystical experience. "I loaf and invite my soul," he writes of the experience; "I lean and loaf at my ease observing a spear of grass...." He then speaks of what he did to enter the experience, Namely, "retiring back" and letting go of his thoughts of "creeds and schools" he entered the Cognitive-Emptying stage of a Divine experience.

I remember experiencing this stage one time while walking along the shoreline of Quanah Parker Lake at the Wichita Mountain Wildlife Refuge in Oklahoma. Emptying my mind of distractions gave rise to a here-and-now experience of nature bursting with a multitude of sensations. It was the first blush of spring when the sun shines through the tender green leaves emerging from their buds. This golden green made the spent grass and leaves of winter recede into the background. The southern wind took the chill off the late afternoon air and dispersed floating pollen from the surrounding trees. As I walked along immersed in the present moment, I became acutely aware of the sensory dance of nature created by the blowing wind. It rhythmically swayed the tall grass bordering the lake and skimmed along the surface of the water, ruffling it, while pushing white popcorn shaped clouds across the sky. As the sun sank lower its color deepened, casting streaks across the sky; it lit up the trees and glittered on the water. This glittering path across the lake seemed to follow me as I walked along the shoreline. The music I was listening to, as well as the wind, helped me, not only to see but also to feel the elements of nature dance in response to the gusts of wind.

Inside, I was experiencing a similar springtime, a freshness of being, unfettered by the debris of my own thinking. I still felt separate from nature, but my experience was not just intellectual; on the contrary, it was wordless and sensory, without distraction or evaluation. My mind was empty, purged. But my senses were open to the world of experience, and then like Wordsworth in *Intimations of Immortality,* I found that "Every common sight to me did seem appareled in celestial light." Or as J. Trevor experienced, the "scene around stood out more clearly" and there was an "illumination in the midst" of where I stood." Dr. Bucke also reported such an illumination experience by a woman he referred to only as C.Y.E. "I left my friend and was walking slowly homeward," he wrote of her experience, "…and simultaneously every object about me became bathed in a soft light, clearer and more ethereal than I had ever before seen." Carl McColman in *The Aspiring Mystic* reports his own experience of mystical light. "Luminous, resplendent, glowing," he writes of the experience, "It's as if everything—the walls of the room, the various people within it, the bread and the wine being passed from hand to hand—shimmered with a light that I could still perceive even when I closed my eyes.

Sometimes a here-and-now experience of the sensory world is so intense that it inspires a sense of gratitude at being able to observe its beauty that can then burst forth into a light rain of love within you. Whitman, poet of both nature and love, describes such an experience in "Song of Myself":

> I mind how once we lay such a transparent summer
>
> Morning, how you settled your head athwart my hips
>
> and gently turn'd over upon me,
>
> And parted the shirt from my bosom-bone, and plunged
>
> Your tongue to my bare-stripped heart.
>
> And reach'd till you felt my beard, and reach'd till you
>
> Held my feet.
>
> Swiftly arose and spread around me the peace and knowledge
>
> That pass all the argument of the earth,
>
> And I know that the hand of God is the promise of my own,
>
> And I know the spirit of God is the brother of my own…

I don't know whether Walt Whitman's experience of love in what I call the Cognitive-Emptying stage is actually tied to his body or he just used concrete sensual words to describe his experience. For me, such love is not connected with my body or the external world. It flows within as the sensory world flows without. In this stage of the encounter, I experience myself as a separate observer of both my inner feeling of love and the flow of the outer sensory world of nature that initially inspired it. This inner flow of love then creates a desire within to join with nature on a deeper level.

In summation, the Cognitive-Emptying Stage of a mystical encounter is attained by applying some form of the Law of Forgiveness to achieve a quiet, empty mind. When we achieve the "Void" or the "Great Silence," we then experience ourselves in the here-and-now as separate but keen observers of the sensory world. Like an antenna we feel the textures, see the sights, and hear the sounds of the world around us. And in the mist of all this sensing, a glistening light appears, illuminating everything around us. In the beauty of this flowing river of illuminated sensations, inner love surfaces and urges us to let go of our sense of separateness and join with the flow of nature on a deeper level. It is this urge to unite with the sensory world of nature that leads us into the next stage of a Divine experience.

I call the second phase of a Divine experience the Sensory-Synchronizing stage because it involves experiencing the unity and order of the sensory world. By keeping our minds empty and following our desire to join with nature, we can let go again using the Law of Forgiveness and experience deeper levels of the sensory world until at some point, we become aware of its underlying unity and order. We can experience the way each sensory element resonates with the others to form a harmonious symphony of sensations. It is this synchronized rhythm in nature that the Hindu poet Rabindranath Tagore celebrates in the poem "Autumn" (cited by R.A. Gilbert in *The Elements of Mysticism*):

> In the stillness I hear in every blade of grass, in
> every speck of dust, in every part of my body, in the
> visible and invisible worlds, in the planets, the sun, and
> the stars, the joyous dance of the atoms through endless
> time—the myriad murmuring waves of rhythm
> surrounding Thy throne.

Many Native American religions evidence knowledge of and promote living in what I am calling the Sensory-Synchronizing stage of Cosmic Surfing. In "Sacred Earth Drums," David and Steve Gordon say that they "hope to inspire others to walk in balance on the Earth Mother who nourishes us." Donald Sandner in *Navaho Symbols of Healing* discusses the Navajos' emphasis on living in harmony with every aspect of nature—the water, the sky, the earth, and other animals. He also cites a speech given by Black Elk, an Oglala Sioux, that shows exquisite sensitivity to the order and unity of nature, which Black Elk expresses in terms of a circle, saying:

> Everything the power of the world does is done in a circle. The sky is round, and I have learned that the earth is round like a ball, and so are all the stars. The wind, in its greatest power, whirls. Birds make their nests in circles, for theirs is the same religion as ours. The sun comes forth and goes down in a circle. The moon does the same, and both are round. Even the seasons form a great circle in their changing, and always come back again to where they were. The life of man is a circle from childhood to childhood, and so it is in everything where power moves. Our tepees were round like the nests of birds, and these were always set in a circle, the nation's hoop, a nest of many nests, where the Great Spirit meant for us to hatch our children.

Clearly Black Elk views nature as ordered, contained, and working in a unified manner.

Ralph Waldo Emerson also described the unity of nature in terms of circles in his essay entitled "Circles." "The eye," he wrote, "is the first circle; the horizon it forms is the second; and throughout nature this primary figure is repeated without end. It is the highest emblem in the cipher of the world. St. Augustine described the nature of God as a circle whose center was everywhere and its circumference nowhere…. around every circle another can be drawn; that there is no end in nature, but every end is a beginning."

Similarly, Carl Jung noted in his psychoanalytic studies of the cultural artifacts of various civilizations that circles repeatedly appear in different forms but always represent the same underlying idea of order, harmony, and wholeness. He called such circles mandalas and believed that they were symbols of wholeness and unity. Jung believed that dreams showed such mandalas as circles, squares, crosses and stars long before people underwent mystical experiences. Seeing and experiencing mandalas within nature during this stage of a Divine encounter may be taken as an indication of an awareness of wholeness that is still enmeshed in the external world of appearances. As such they can be considered signposts on our inner journey to reach the Divine within.

While actually circling a campfire at Kodachrome State Park in southwestern Utah, I had a particularly powerful experience of such unity and order in nature. At dusk I built a campfire and the wood I gathered for the fire was so dry that it crackled as it burst into flames when I tossed a match on it. I sat listening to my "Sacred Spirits I" CD and looking at the fire. It burned bright and hot forming a vibrant ball of flames that appeared to bounce up and down on the red desert ground. As I watched the ball of fire dance, felt its heat, smelled its smoke, and listened to the wood snapping and popping and to the chants of Native Americans on my CD player, I began focusing my awareness on first one, then another of the elements of this desert scene. My attention shifted from the bouncing sphere of fire to the red sandy earth and then to the surrounding clumps of desert grass and the silvery green sage bushes standing tall in the moonlight. I could feel the dry sand under my feet just waiting for water to bloom with life. I saw the clumps of green desert grass as they shimmered and rippled in the desert wind and noted the surrounding silvery green sage bushes, which could only bend stiffly in it.

I realized that each of the elements around me formed a unified, self-contained system with its own unique sensory qualities of size, shape, texture, color, and flexibility. I could sense and feel the internal unity within each of these elements. It then dawned on me that although each of these elements was unified within itself and formed its own territory of existence, it was also unified with the surrounding elements in the desert. And with that realization, the unity of the world of nature gushed forth into my mind. I suddenly understood and could actually feel its unity in the harmonious blending of its elements.

Nature is not a cacophony of disunited elements. Light, for instance, does not war with darkness; rather it dispels it at dawn. But what about nighttime, when darkness dispels light? This question opened my mind to the idea that there must be some type of order operating within the world of nature. I realized that nature not only has unity, it also has order. In the case of light and darkness there is an order in which one recedes while the other becomes dominant. While sitting by the campfire, I became aware of the movement of the world around me. "Yes," I thought, "to every thing there is a season, and a time to every purpose under the heaven" (Ecclesiastes 3:1). The unity and order of nature permeated my awareness; I could feel its harmony within me. It was one of those magical moments, and suddenly I wanted to move with the experience, so I got up and began walking around the campfire. As I circled the fire, I began to feel as if the Native American chanters on the CD were actually there with me in the desert forming a circle of humanity moving around the flames. I then joined with the unity and order that I perceived in the desert. Sights, sounds, and movements all blended together, forming a harmonious symphony of synchronized sensations. I lingered in this experience until dawn, then I drifted into sleep.

During the next phase of the Sensory-Synchronizing stage of a mystical experience of the Divine, an awareness of the infinite nature of the world surfaces into consciousness. "Every particle of the world is a mirror," writes Mahmud Shabestari in a poem cited by Andrew Harvey in *The Essential Mystics* "in each atom lies the blazing light of a thousand suns." The poems continues:

> Cleave the heart of a raindrop,
>
> a hundred pure oceans will flow forth.
>
> Look closely at a grain of sand,
>
> the seed of a thousand beings can be seen.
>
> The foot of an ant is larger than an elephant;
>
> in essence, a drop of water is no different
>
> than the Nile.
>
> In the heart of a barley corn lies the fruit
>
> of a hundred harvests;

within the pulp of a millet seed

an entire universe can be found.

In the wing of a fly, an ocean of wonder;

in the pupil of the eye, an endless heaven.

Though the inner chamber of the heart is small,

the Lord of both worlds gladly makes his

home there

In Shabestari's poem, we can easily see that the celebration of infinity is still immersed within the sensory world of nature.

We can also experience this sense of the infinite in nature by expanding our awareness of the unity and order in the nature immediately around us. After becoming aware of the synchronized unity of nature, we can direct our consciousness to continually expand until we reach a sense of the infinite unity and order of the universe. At Kodachrome State Park, after I had experienced the harmony and order between the elements around my campfire, I directed my mind to let go so that my awareness expanded to include more and more elements of nature. My awareness of the still desert landscape grew to include awareness of the moon circling the world, the world circling the solar system, and the blanket of stars covering the heavens. I was aware of the order in it all, and a gentle stream of love flowed within me. I still felt separate from the world, but now, I could surf with my mind from the finite unity and order of my immediate present surroundings to a sense of the infinite unity and order of the universe far beyond. What a mental ride!

On most occasions after an awareness of the infinity quality of nature emerges, I experience myself as a small, finite observer of the infinite but harmonious, orderly world of nature. In the Sensory-Synchronizing Stage, we still experience ourselves as separate from the unity and order of nature as well as from a sense of its infinite nature. The experience of unity and order in the Sensory-Synchronizing stage can become so intense that it leads many seekers to believe that there is a Divine principle behind nature holding its elements together for some purpose. Others draw a line at this point and do not go any further in their journey. They prefer to stay in the "murmuring waves of rhythm surrounding Thy throne" that Tagore spoke of in his poem "Autumn." Many consider the notion of God or some Divine reality as unnecessary or just some aspect of nature, nothing more. But there is a danger that such beliefs may become self-fulfilling prophecies in which our conclusion that God doesn't exist becomes a premise that excludes the Divine and thereby prevents experiencing other stages of a Divine experience.

The Sensory-Synchronizing Stage ends with a feeling that everything-is-as-it-should-be—that nothing needs to be said, thought, or done. We feel about the world as Robert Browning felt in "Pippa Passes" when he wrote,

> the year's at the spring and day's at the morn;
>
> morning's at seven; the hillside's dew-pearled;
>
> the lark's on the wing; the snail's on the thorn:
>
> God's in his heaven— all's right with the world!

This here-and-now experience of everything-is-as-it-should-be can be conceptualized as a movement from the masculine to the feminine mode of activity. Rather than thinking and feeling something needs to be done—the masculine mode of activity—we make a shift to the feeling that everything-is-as-it-should-be; everything is waxing and waning; everything can be allowed to just exist—the feminine mode of activity. This experience of everything-is-as-it- should-be is one of calm existence in the here and now and signals the end of the Sensory-Synchronizing Stage of an encounter with the Divine.

In both the Cognitive-Emptying and Sensory-Synchronizing stages discussed above, we experience a vividness and brightness permeating nature much like Wordsworth's "celestial light" in "Intimations of Immortality." This stage also culminates in an experience of inner love, but it is more intense than in the prior Cognitive-Emptying stage. Such increased awareness of our inner love in turn creates a stronger desire to join with nature on a deeper level, thereby impelling us onward toward the next stage of a Divine experience.

I call the third stage of a Divine encounter the Kinesthetic-Cognitive stage. Although scientists have classified the kinesthetic feedback from our bodies as one of our basic senses, I include it in this stage rather than the Sensory-Synchronizing Stage because it involves a shift in awareness from the outer world of nature to the inner world of our minds and bodies. The Kinesthetic-Cognitive Stage begins with a longing to unite with nature rather than remain separate from it and then proceeds to an experience of surfing or flowing with the sensory world of experience. It ends with a sense of "at-onement" or oneness with nature and in some cases identification with nature and a loss of self-awareness.

This stage goes through two distinct phases in turning our attention inward and away from the external sensory world. During the kinesthetic phase, we shift our awareness to the inner world of kinesthetic feedback—how our bodies feel on the inside. How our feet feel from within as they touch the ground when we walk. How our arms feel from the inside as we move around in the world. How our chests feel from within when we breathe in and out. Tolle stresses the importance of first becoming aware of our inner bodies in our journey to an experience with the Divine. "The inner body lies at the threshold between your form identity and your essence identity your true nature," he writes. Highly extroverted people are often unaware of their inner kinesthetic world—unaware, that is, of themselves from the inside, so the Kinesthetic-Cognitive Stage may be more difficult for them to achieve. I had a patient once who remarked when trying to gain an awareness of her kinesthetic sense that she had not known that she had an existence inside of herself prior to trying to find it.

Once we have gained awareness of our body, we can apply the principle of forgiveness and let go of our inner kinesthetic or bodily experience and thereby join with the world of nature. We can then use the Alexander Technique to direct our bodies to let go and join with the external world while walking around in it. With this joining, we will experience ourselves as small, finite parts moving with the world of nature. We are no longer just passive observers of the external world; we experience ourselves as moving in a part-whole relationship with it. We are flowing with the sensory world. We are united with nature and feel "at-one" with the earth, sky, trees, grass, and wind. We have hitched a ride with the "myriad murmuring waves surrounding Thy throne." Our bodies are surfing the sensory waves of nature. However, our ride is not complete because our minds still feel separate from this flow.

When we recognize that our emptied minds are separate and long to unite with our bodies, our senses, and the external world, we enter the cognitive phase of this stage of a Divine encounter. This cognitive stage is different from the Cognitive-Emptying Stage because it involves letting our minds join with our bodies and the world rather than simply emptying them of their contents. Again, by applying the Law of Forgiveness, we can let our minds join with our bodies and with the world. But oddly enough, now we don't feel restricted in the body or immersed in the world as we do in holding relationships; rather, we feel free and whole. The world becomes clear, vivid, luminous, and new– as William James describes in *Varieties of Religious Experience*. "I shouted for joy," he writes, at having achieved this state, "I praised God with my whole heart...I remember this, that everything looked new to me, the people, the fields, the cattle, the trees. I was like a new man in a new world." He then goes on to describe an experience of unity with the world: "I felt myself one," he writes, "with the grass, the trees, the birds, insects, everything in nature."

At this point, James was experiencing a complete surf with the sensory world, and so are we. Both our minds and bodies surf the harmonious symphony of sensations. We feel expanded and move at one with the world of appearances. Our sense of oneness with nature can become so intense that we experience the things of nature as ourselves. We can actually lose our self-awareness in this casting off of our separation from nature and instead become completely identified with it. As often as I have had this experience, it has happened to me only a few times. But I know what it is like to feel oneness with a leaf slowly sifting down to the grass and to be a pebble washed over by the cool water of a brook. Once, watching a bird fly across the sky, I joined with it in its flight. I became the bird. I lost all sense of separateness and actually felt the inner movement of its wings in flight. This sense of complete identification with nature is suggested by a number of mystics and poets. "I am the wind that breathes upon the sea," writes a poet in the ancient *Welsh Black Book of Carmarthen*, quoted by Andrew Harvey:

> I am the wave on the ocean,
> I am the murmur of leaves rustling,
> I am the rays of the sun,
> I am the beam on the moon and stars,
> I am power of trees growing,
> I am the bud breaking into blossom,
> I am the movement of the salmon swimming,
> I am the courage of the wild boar fighting,
> I am the speed of the stag running,
> I am the strength of the ox pulling the plough,
> I am the size of the mighty oak tree,
> And I am the thoughts of all people
> Who praise my beauty and grace…

R. A. Gilbert in *The Elements of Mysticism* saw an "ecstatic identification with nature" in the writings of Rumi, a great poet and teacher of Sufism, the mystical branch of Islam.

> I am the dust in the sunlight, I am the ball of the sun,
> To the dust I say: Remain. And to the sun, roll on.
> I am the mist of morning. I am the breath of evening.
> I am the rustling of the grove, the surging wave of the sea.
> I am the mast, the rudder, the steersman and the ship.
> I am the coral reef on which it founders.
> I am the tree of life and the parrot in its branches,
> Silence, thought, tongue and voice.
> I am the breath of the flute, the spirit of man,
> I am the spark in the stone, the gleam of gold in metal.

The candle and the moth fluttering round it,
The rose and the nightingale drunk with its fragrance.
I am the chain of being, the circle of the spheres.
The scale of creation, the rise and the fall.
I am what is and is not. I am—O Thou who knowest,
Jalaluddin, oh say it—I am the soul in all.

And, of course, Walt Whitman evidences such an expanded identification with nature in "Song of Myself":

Sea of stretch'd ground-swells,
Sea breathing broad and convulsive breaths,
Sea of the brine of life and of unshovell'd
Yet always-ready graves,
Howler and scooper of storms,
Capricious and dainty sea,
I am integral with you, I too
Am of one phase and of all phases.

People first experiencing a loss of self-identification with nature may find the experience to be very frightening. But with time, such fear diminishes and is replaced with an influx of love for all of nature.

I think that these first three stages of Cosmic Surfing not only show a shift from the masculine mode of activity to the feminine mode, but also illustrate what many philosophers and Eastern religions mean by transcending the subject/object dichotomy. This idea refers to the fact that we see ourselves, the subject, as separate from the external world, which is considered to be the object. According to some Eastern religions, thinking is what separates us from a sense of oneness and causes the subject/object dichotomy. Thus, we have to suspend the thinking mind to undo or transcend the subject/object dichotomy and regain our sense of oneness. For this reason, Eastern religions advocate meditation and the use of koans to undo the activity of our thinking minds. Again, these techniques are all based on the principle of forgiveness or letting go to achieve states of unity and oneness.

The Existential philosopher Kierkegaard stated that we cannot transcend the subject/object dichotomy and become one with the Divine unless our faith is focused on what is truly ultimate. He defined faith as the state of being "ultimately concerned" and believed that if our faith were focused on something less than the ultimate, we would be consumed. For example, if our ultimate concern is only money, then we will be consumed by money and unable to transcend the subject/object dichotomy and achieve a sense of wholeness. His point is similar to the one I have made about holding relationships. If we hold on to people, things, and actions in the world, then we maintain our separation from the Divine within; our holding relationships consume us.

If we deny the existence of the Divine or see nature as God, we may become fixated in these first three stages and never experience the other stages because of our self-fulfilling beliefs about the Divine. Simply put, if we don't believe in the Divine, then our beliefs can serve to block any evidence or experiences that are spiritual. For example, if we did not believe that trees exist, then we would never experience them—we would not see, hear, smell or feel them. Even if we walked into a tree and fell down, we would associate the experience with something other than a tree, a shoe problem or possibly the fact that we were just clumsy and fell.

Alternatively, we can believe in the Divine but remain fixated in these first stages of Cosmic Surfing because we try to put All Being into a material box. We attempt to concretize God and ensnare the Divine within the natural world. I once had a patient who hesitantly told me that she wanted to have sex with God. She felt guilty and frightened by this thought. I explained to her that she was simply concretizing her love for God and experiencing it within the world of nature. I then showed her how to free her love for God from the enmeshment with bodily sensations. It seems to me that to identify the Divine with nature or to exalt nature to godhood in this stage is to form a holding relationship that would prevent a connection with the Divine. Many Eastern religions maintain that nature is "Maya" or illusion. If it is, then not to move onward after identifying with it is to be satisfied with an illusion. Augustine writes in *Confessions*,

I asked the earth and it answered me: 'I am not it' and all
things whatsoever in it made the same confession. I asked the sea
and the deeps and the creeping things and they answered me: "We
are not thy God; seek beyond us"...
I asked the heavens, the sun and moon and stars: 'Nor,' say they, 'are
we the God thou seekest.

Augustine clearly believes that the Divine lies beyond the world of
nature. But it is important to join with nature as a step in our journey
toward an experience of the Divine.

During the first three stages of a Divine encounter, then, we
move from being passive observers of the world around us to joining
and surfing with the harmonious flow of the sensory world. In the
Cognitive-Emptying stage, we experience ourselves as being in the here-
and-now as observers, not surfers, of the sensory flow of nature. In the
Sensory-Synchronizing Stage, we are still passive observers, but now
we become aware of the unity, order and infinite nature of the sensory
world. This stage ends with a sense that everything-is-as-it-should-be.
During the Kinesthetic-Cognitive Stage, we join and then flow with
the harmonious of the sensory world. If we let go while experiencing
oneness with nature during the Kinesthetic-Cognitive stage, we enter
the next phase of a Divine encounter, which I call the Being stage. Here
we encounter the external world in a new way.

In the Being stage of the Divine encounter, unlike the earlier stages,
we do not always experience the external world as unified, orderly, or
in a state of everything-is-as-it-should-be. In fact, during this stage the
world of nature can take on an animated quality in which we can see
faces in clouds, trees, rocks, and leaves. It's as if the appearance of nature
is no longer perceived as an objective, separate dimension. Instead, we
look at the world through the eyes of Being or the Divine within, not
through the lens of science or the subject/object dichotomy.

Many of my earliest mystical experiences involved seeing faces in
clouds and trees. Some appeared as different manifestations of Jesus
while the other faces were unknown to me. To have these experiences,
I would sit quietly at Lake Waco, usually during a sunset. I turned my

attention inward and then directed my mind to let go until I saw nature become animated with faces. I did not fully understand the genesis of these experiences then but sought them for the pleasure and delight they brought me. At the time I considered them to be the ultimate religious experience, but later, of course, I realized that they were only a small part of a more powerful mystical process. Eventually, however, these experiences became so intense that they alarmed me and I began to avoid them altogether. This happened while I was driving back to Texas after a Christmas vacation in the early 1970s. I was on the highway just outside of Atlanta, Georgia when a vast face appeared in the clouds of a sunset. As I stared into the eyes of this face it suddenly opened, and I felt the spirit of love behind this image connect with the love within me. I remember thinking at the time that this must be the spirit of Christ, but I was frightened nevertheless.

Many years later—about a year after his death in May of 2002—I saw a side view of my father in a large cloud. I was sitting on a sun-warmed boulder on the shoreline of Quanah Parker Lake in the Wichita Mountain Wildlife Refuge in Oklahoma. As I scanned the sage and yellow green patches of lichen surrounding its sides, across the shining dark lake, and then up into the clear blue sky above it, I spotted several big white clouds slowly drifting by. As I let go and focused on one of them, it reconfigured into my father's face. There was no mistaking this image, it included the slightly mischievous smile that was always present in the right corner of his mouth. As I looked at this image, I could feel my father's spirit and my old connection to him. Unlike the experience outside of Atlanta, this one was not frightening. On the contrary, I felt grateful for it. Then, as quickly as he had come, my father's face disappeared and I watched the cloud's retreat over the red sloping hills surrounding the lake.

More recently, while hiking the floor of Canyon de Chelly in the Navajo land of Arizona, I commented to my Navajo guide that the canyon was like a beautiful cathedral carved by the hands of God. Very matter-of-factly he said yes, and added, "Just look at the faces of spirits in the surrounding rocks and trees." He then pointed to one small boulder above us and said, "That one has many spirit faces in it."

A single glance at this rock confirmed his observation and reminded me of other times that I had seen such competing spirit faces in other places and did not realize what they were. As we continued our hike to Spider Rock, I reflected on my initial fear at seeing spirit faces in nature, and Texas', my Navajo guide, matter-of-fact attitude toward them and chuckle at myself.

When we first move into the Being stage, our prior sense of oneness with nature can also flower into an experience of nature's multidimensionality. If we continue to apply the principle of forgiveness and let go while feeling "at-one" with nature, we break through the bonds of the sensory world and become aware of an inner dimension underlying the world and ourselves. We feel the depth of nature. First our awareness extends beyond the appearance of things outside of ourselves. We can sense and feel the inward invisible spirit behind the outward visible sign. We become aware of the breath of life behind the world of nature. "You can feel God-essence in every creature, every flower, every stone," Eckhart writes about such an ecstatic experience, "and you realize all that is, is holy." He goes on to cite Jesus from the Gospel of St. Thomas: "Split a piece of wood; I am there, "lift a stone, and you will find me there." Bucke reports a similar experience by Jacob Boehme, a German shoemaker, had at the age of twenty-five. "But here he remarked that he gazed into the very heart of things," he writes, "the very herbs and grass, and that actual nature harmonized with what he had inwardly seen."

Now if we broaden our awareness by including more and more of the world around us, then at a certain point in this expansion of our minds we suddenly become aware that this inner dimensional aspect or depth of nature is infinite. And if we close our eyes and let go, we can experience the oneness with Being that Buddha spoke of in his teachings. While staying at Spiderwoman Campground in the Navajo lands of Arizona, I experienced such wholeness. I was sitting cross-legged in front of a fire of cedar and pinion wood listening to some Native American chanting. I closed my eyes when an awareness of the depth and dimension of nature arose in my mind and then let go so as

95

to join the universe. When my consciousness returned to me I knew that I had had an experience of wholeness or at-onement.

We can also experience light emanating within these many dimensions of nature like that seen in multifaceted gems. This would not be surprising to Paramahansa Yogananda, a Hindu yogi and founder of the Self-Realization Fellowship in America, in *Autobiography of a Yogi* he asserts that light is the essential structure of the universe. He quotes Genesis: "Let there be light: and there was light," as a spiritual source for his belief that "the universe as the Lord created it is an essential undifferentiated mass of light." Yogananda points out that light has been found to make up the most fundamental aspect of matter. He observes that in physics matter is now considered to be composed of electrons having a dual nature, that is, consisting of both particles or matter and waves or light. So whether we view creation with an electron microscope or surf with our minds beyond the material world and connect with Being behind the appearance of things, it is hardly surprising that we encounter radiating light.

One of my earliest encounters with this light at the heart of nature occurred for me just after my brother's death in 1979. It was a cold day and the land surrounding Lake Waco was covered with a fresh blanket of snow. I was walking along the shoreline enjoying the solitude of this white wonderland. It struck me that the blanket of snow seemed to unite the water, rocks, trees, and sky into a harmonious living whole, and when it did, a recognition of the inherent order and unity of nature as a whole overwhelmed me; suddenly, I felt an urge to embrace the world around me. I reached out to a tall bush beside me encased in its drape of ice and snow—and when I touched it, I realized that it felt like my brother's cold hand as he had lain in his coffin. At that moment, I was transported into a multidimensional experience. I was still acutely aware of the sensory world around me, but now I was also aware of its infinite depth, its infinite multidimensional aspect. It was as if the sensory world had been flat or one dimensional a moment before, but now it stretched into infinity and eternity. Although I was walking around the lake in real time, I was clearly experiencing the Being or "breath of life" pulsating behind the world of appearances.

The snow–covered rocks, trees, grass, and bushes around me were multidimensional and singing with life. As the song "Jesus Christ Superstar" says the "rocks and stones themselves begin to sing." And the thought occurred to me that plants, rocks, trees, and bushes all lived in a continual state of Being and that I might really be at the bottom of the phylogenetic tree while they were really at the top. I then found to my surprise and delight that I felt as close to these seemingly inanimate objects as I normally do to animals. I felt love for every living thing and connected to everything. Reflecting on that and subsequent, similar experiences, I can now understand why many Native American and Eastern religions show such respect for not just the sentient but also the nonsentient beings of nature.

All of nature seemed to be permeated with Being and flowing with the "breath of life" blown by Wakan Tanka, the Great Spirit. I sat down to embrace the moment and built a small fire to warm myself. As I placed my hands over the fire, not only could I feel its heat, I could also sense its depth, the extension of Being behind its appearance. As I expanded my mind to include more of the world, I eventually became aware of the infinite nature of this dimensional experience. And the light illuminated all around me filling these dimensions with a splendid brightness. The experience was so moving that I went back to the lake for several days in an effort to recapture it, but, like the snow, it melted away into a memory.

Now if we apply the Law of Forgiveness and let go while experiencing the infinite dimensional nature of the world, surprisingly we can surf to deeper levels within ourselves. While warming my hands over the fire at Lake Waco and allowing my mind to expand outward until I experienced the infinite dimensional aspect or depth of nature, a shift suddenly took place in my mind, and I became aware of my inner being. At the very place where I became fully aware of it, my mental surf outward to infinity turned inward into a realization of the "I am that I am" that lies within us and behind everything in the world.

When we reach this inner point, we have reached the "breath of life" or the Divine within that Jung calls the Self and Buddhists call the nonattached mind. According to Jung, the Self is the unifying and organizing principle in our psyches that produces a sense of wholeness. He maintains that we project the Self outward into the external world of nature. When we surf inward to this point in our minds, we realize that the unity and order experienced in the Sensory-Synchronizing stage, the oneness with nature experienced in the Kinesthetic-Cognitive stage, and the multidimensional experience in the early part of the Being stage lie within us and not in the external world of nature. We now feel connected more to our inner being than to the outer world of nature. This is the place where we experience ourselves as a still point in a turning world. It is here that we feel connected to everyone and everything. When we identify ourselves solely in terms of the outer world of appearances and our holding relationships with it, we will feel isolated and alone. But when we join with the Being within ourselves that is beyond the world of appearances, we will feel connected to all things, sentient and nonsentient. We feel a part of the Great River of Life that flows behind the world we see and feel.

If we let go while experiencing the depth and multidimensionality of the world and ourselves, we will encounter the pure light of the Being stage. Robert May cites Zev ben Shimon Halevi, a modern Kabbalist who states that "When a person comes into the presence of God …they come into the presence of the light, the world of light." The Kabbala, the text of Jewish mysticism, calls the Godhead "Ain Sof Aur," which means literally "limitless light." I think the interface or door where the material and spiritual worlds meet is where we experience the "Clear Light." If we turn in one direction we return to the world of appearances, but if we go in the opposite direction, we enter the spiritual world of the Being stage and the pure light. When we look at a prism, we see pure light on one side and a rainbow of colors on the other side. The prism itself is like the interface or door between these two planes of existence. Many religions speak of the light within that we encounter when we let go of the world of appearances and of our holding relationships with it. In Christianity, Matthew 6:22 says, "If, therefore, thine eye be single, thy whole body shall be full of light." Similarly, Yogananda says "A yogi who through perfect meditation has merged his consciousness with the Creator perceives the cosmic essence as light (vibrations of light energy)." W.Y. Evans-Wentz in *The Tibetan Book of the Dead* noted that Buddhists believe that when we let go of the world at the moment of death we come "face to face with the fundamental Clear Light." By uniting with the Clear Light, it is thought that we can obtain liberation from the cycle of birth and death. Evans-Wentz also remarked that recognition of the Clear Light by saints and mystics of the West resulted in an "ecstatic condition of consciousness" called "Illumination." More recently, Raymond Moody in *Life After Life* has detailed the experiences of patients who returned after dying. Most reported that they left their bodies, traveled through a tunnel away from the world of appearances and entered a world of light and love.

Not only is light associated with leaving the world of appearances and entering the world of Being, it also occurs in the opposite direction when we leave the spiritual world and enter the world of appearances. Bryan Walsh, the author and manager of a web site detailing the apparitions of Mary, cites many examples in which the Virgin Mary is said to have appeared in a blaze or globe of white light. One such apparition occurred in April of 1968 when more than a million people saw Mary's appearance broadcast on Egyptian TV and photographed by hundreds of photographers. She appeared at St. Mary's Coptic Church in Zietum, Egypt in the land of the pyramids. Her apparitions lasted from a few minutes to as long as nine hours for about three years. These appearances were of a woman surrounded by a very bright globe of light and accompanied by doves of light.

Quantum theory suggests an explanation for why light appears when we enter and leave the world in the Being stage. It has to do with moving from a lower to a higher vibration or energy level. Jason Stephenson in *Quantum Physics for Beginners: Quantum Mechanics and Quantum Theory Explained* states that electrons tend to give off light whenever their speed is increased or decreased. When an electron drops from a higher to a lower orbit it loses energy and the atom containing that electron emits light which carries off the lost energy. We experience this as being in a lower or deflated vibratory state. When we have a religious experience, we are going to a higher vibration and gaining light. I had an experience of increased light while doing a sunset meditation at Lake

Ray Hubbard in Rowlett, Texas. After reading Jonathan Goldman's book called the *Divine Name*, I took the instructional CD that came with the book to the lake to practice intoning the sound of the Divine name and thereby experience changes in my physical body and energy fields.

It was hot evening with the temperature above 100 degrees so I was the only person at the lake. I began intoning with the voice on the CD and after about 20 minutes a huge swarm of flying insects surrounded me. I stopped intoning the Divine name because I did not want to inhale these insects. To my surprise, the insects left immediately so I started intoning the Divine name again and the insects immediately returned so I stopped again for fear of choking if I inhaled them. Again, the insects left and this time, my curiosity was elicited. So I began to experiment to see if, in fact, there was a relationship between intoning and the presence of these insects and indeed there was a relationship. It was getting dark by this time and when the street lights at the lake came on, I glanced at them and saw insects flying around the lights. When I saw this, a light came on in my mind and an inner voice said, "Insects are phototropic meaning they are attracted to light so the insects swarming you were drawn to the light that surrounded you when you were intoning the Divine name." What an experience this was to me!

Now if we let go and join with the Light of our Being, we will experience ourselves as light. The "celestial light" that we observed outside of ourselves in earlier stages of Cosmic Surfing we now experience as part of our own inner being. Burke reported that during one of his mystical experiences "he knew the light was within him." He also cited an experience that St John of the Cross had following a "dark night of the soul" when he saw a light "so brilliant…that for two or three days afterwards…his eyes were weak, as if he had been looking at the sun in its strength."

During my first sweat lodge experience, I became acutely aware of my own inner light. Many Native Americans conduct purification and religious ceremonies in oval or round structures called sweat lodges that consist of a frame of saplings covered with skins, canvas, or blankets. A shallow pit for heated rocks is dug in the center and water containing various herbs is thrown on the rocks to create steam. The ceremony is conducted in complete darkness by a medicine man who prays, chants, and sings. To my surprise, about an hour into the ceremony, I noticed what seemed to be a flashlight suddenly coming on inside the sweat lodge. I looked around to see where the light was coming from and then a voice in my mind said, "The light is in you and I realized that the light was in my own mind. I then felt a trickle of fear in my stomach but quickly let it go and smiled with delight at my new realization.

The many biblical references to Jesus as the "Light of the world" suggest that he reached this level of the Being stage or at least that the authors of the Gospels knew of the light and saw it in him. In the Gospel of St. Thomas as reported by James Robinson in *The Nag Hammadi Library*, Jesus said, "If they say to you, 'Where did you come from?' say to them, 'We came from the light, the place where the light came into being."

The teachings of *A Course in Miracles* include discussions of the Great Rays of God that extend as sparks of light in each of us. "Turn toward the light," it says, "for the little spark in you is part of a Light so great that it can sweep you out of all darkness forever." The Hindu religion in the puja ceremony also indicates an awareness of the inner light that I associate with this stage of a Divine encounter. And the Hindu celebration of Diwali includes this ceremony that involves the adherents symbolically taking away ignorance by illuminating themselves with light. By passing the hand over a fire, they believe that they can take on its light, and then by rubbing the head with it, they can remove ignorance and be illuminated. Tulku Thondup, a Tibetan Buddhist, also describes such experiences of light in *Enlightened Journey*:

When I said "light", you probably thought about beams of light Or sunlight like phenomena coming from somewhere. But in true realization you are not realizing those lights as objects—the objects of the eye consciousness and so forth. You are realizing the light as clarity and luminosity, which is also peace, joy, bliss, openness, and all-knowing wisdom. And you are the light and the light is you, oneness. This is the union of openness nature (emptiness) and the spontaneously arising wisdom and appearances (Intrinsic light). This principle is the very basis from which esoteric Buddhism speaks of nonduality, natural light, clarity, spontaneously arising, spontaneously present, simultaneous awareness, self-arisen, unborn, and fully enlightened... That light was not just the light of our ideas, but the light of feeling, the light of experiences, the light of peace and bliss, but is beyond description, time, and dimensions. So even the people who have near death experiences have some glimpse of pure light.

The experience of being the light and the light's being you ushers in a number of emotions. Upon realizing "the light was within him," Bucke in the introduction to *Cosmic Consciousness* reported that he experienced "a sense of exultation, of immense joyousness accompanied or immediately followed by an intellectual illumination quite impossible to describe." I have found that first there is joy and delight at feeling the "breath of life," followed by a sense of satisfaction at arriving in Being stage. This satisfaction is like a sense of having come closer to what is your real home and hearth. There is also a depth of gratitude and a desire to give it expression. Finally, a deep love for the Divine surfaces and dispels inner fears, just like the Gospel of John says it does: "Perfect love casts out fear" (I John 4:18).

It is from this still point of illuminated Being within that we let go and join with the Great River of Life—the Zero Energy Field. Just as we let go to join the sensory world of appearances, we can let go and join a state of Being beyond the world of appearances. My first experience of joining the Great River of Life occurred during my graduate school years in Waco, Texas. At the time I was dating a philosophy major and we would go to Lake Waco on a Friday or Saturday night alone or sometimes with other couples. There, we would build a big fire, listen to music, and have long philosophical discussions with our dinner and wine. One evening, while lying on a pebbled peninsula of the lake, looking up at the star-studded heaven, and listening to the Moody Blues album "In Search of the Lost Cord," I suddenly felt as though I was moving in space. It felt as though the pebbled beach had morphed into a magic carpet sailing with the universe. It was a wonderful experience, but I discounted it as due to the effects of the wine and the music. It was nearly thirty years later when I became fully aware that this experience, along with others was part of a mystical process.

This aspect of the Being stage of Cosmic Surfing is very active even though during it we may be lying on the ground looking up through the leafy canopy of a tree or ambling around the rim of a desert canyon. It also has a great feeling of being free and unbounded by the sensory world. One evening, while I was watching a sunset at Lake Ray Hubbard near my home in Texas, I entered the Being stage. As I sat on the rocky shoreline listening to a CD by Douglas Spotted Eagle entitled "Closer to Far Away", I turned inward and began to let go. I emptied my mind and let my body relax. Soon I was experiencing the order and harmony of the world around me. With another direction to let go, I began surfing this sensory world. I flowed with its colors, its textures, and its forms. The warm southerly wind brushing across my skin heightened my experience of movement. As my attention moved from the deep orange setting sun to the choppy waves of the lake, I suddenly shot through the sensory world and into a multidimensional experience and became aware of its inner depth. I felt the Being behind the appearance of things. Both sentient and nonsentient beings were teeming with life. This awareness grew until my consciousness abruptly shifted inward and I became more aware of my inner being. I then felt as though I was light and inwardly luminous.

When I let go again, I felt a faint sense of delight and then a surge of joy as I begin to move with the Great Spirit. I was surfing the Cosmos. As I surfed deeper into the "breath of life," a sense of gratitude for my unique creation and existence swelled up in me. It was not tainted by the narcissism or grandiosity of a puffed up or inflated ego; it was a genuine thankfulness to God for creating me. As I watched the dancing waves on the lake, I knew that each one was unique, yet, also joined with all the other waves to form a moving body of water. I felt aware of my own uniqueness, too, and enormously grateful for it, but at the same time, I felt connected to all Being or the Spirit of the Cosmos. I felt eternity and infinity unbounded by the sensory world. I felt the light of my Being. With this sense of gratitude, love washed over me and created an intense desire for a personal encounter with the Divine.

The Being stage of a mystical experience represents a full shift from the masculine mode of activity of doing, competing, and heading toward goals that we live in everyday life to the feminine mode of being, allowing, and letting nature take its course. We begin the Being stage with a sense of the order, unity, and oneness of things that at first seems external but that we soon realize actually lies within. We move from feeling joy and delight in response to nature to feeling gratitude and love for the Divine. The here-and-now and everything-is-as-it-should-be experiences associated with previous stages become an experience of the eternity and infinity of Being behind the world of nature. When we have fully connected with the Being within us, we no longer feel isolated or alone. We feel connected with the Eye of the Great Spirit and the Great River of Life. We end this stage with an experience of the light or luminosity of our Being, surfing with the Spirit of Life, and with an intense longing for a more complete union with the Divine, for there is still a sense that something is lacking and that we have not completely connected with the Divine, the heart of everything. We long to join with the Source of love. We yearn for the heart of God. "I have only one desire to feel you close beside me, as did Moses on the peak of Sinai," wrote Amir Hamzah in "One Alone." He captured this hunger for the personal love of the Divine.

I call the fifth stage of a mystical experience of the Divine the Receiving stage because it involves experiencing a personal connection with the Divine, thereby receiving the heart of God. By applying the Law of Forgiveness at the end of the Being stage, we are opening our hearts to receive a personal heart felt encounter with the Divine. Buddha experienced a state of nonattachment or Universal Being but not a personal heart felt relationship with God. The teachings of Muslims, Jews, and Christians, all emphasize a personal helping relationship with a Divine Being. The devout Muslim reads in the Qu'ran, "God wants to clarify you and guide you…to lighten your burden." The Psalms of the Old Testament lay out what God has done for the Jewish people, what

He will do for them in the future, and the need for Him in the present. Psalm 23:1-4 illustrates the Jewish belief in a personal relationship with God.

> The Lord is my shepherd; I shall not want.
> He maketh me to lie down in green pastures: he
> leadeth me beside the still waters.
> He restoreth my soul: he leadeth me in the paths
> of righteousness for his name's sake.
> Yea, though I walk through the valley of the shadow
> of death, I will fear no evil: for thou art with me;
> thy rod and thy staff they comfort me...

St. Paul defines the Christian's relationship with God as that of a father to a child:

> The Spirit beareth witness with our spirit,
> that we are the children of God;
> and if children, then heirs—heirs of God, and
> joint heirs with Christ ...
> Romans 8: 16-17."

By letting go or applying the principle of forgiveness, we can open ourselves to a personal relationship with the Divine and ultimately receive the heart of God. In *A Return to Love*, Marianne Williamson calls us to reconnect with the love within us. With the author of *A Course in Miracles*, she believes that "The spiritual journey is the relinquishment, or unlearning of fear, and the acceptance of love back into our hearts." In *Practicing His Presence*, Brothers Lawrence and Laubach talk about making a conscious effort to bring God into their minds all day long. Brother Laubach found that reading endless scripture did not bring him into an experience of God, but the mental discipline of consciously inviting God into his mind ultimately did. Both monks focused on bringing God into everyday life by consciously directing the mind to include awareness of him in daily activities. But Brother Lawrence recognized that we have to let go to receive God into our awareness. "Strain," he writes, "does not seem to do good. At the moment I feel something "let go" inside, lo, God is here! It is a heart-melting 'hereness,' a lovely whispering of father to child, and the reason I did not have it before, was because I failed to let go." And of course letting go is the activity associated with the Law of Forgiveness.

To receive the heart of God, we simply apply the principle of forgiveness during the Being stage when we are surfing the Cosmos and experiencing our inner light. By letting go at this point, we are undoing the holding relationships that separate us from the Divine and opening the door to receive the heart of God. The loving desire for God that arose in the Being stage now climaxes in a type of spiritual orgasm in which we feel not only our love for God but also His love for us. It is an ecstatic love that lights our entire being and far transcends any physical pleasures. In *The Aspiring Mystic*, Carl McColman also found that experiences of Divine love far exceed those of ordinary life. He writes "To immediately feel the pulsation of pure joy and passion flood your bones and veins … makes the pleasures of such things as drugs or even sex seem pale and insignificant."

I have received the heart of God many times over the years. On one occasion, I was hiking from Mustang Park back to Bearcat Campground at Benbrook Lake near Fort Worth when the love of God flooded my being. The sun was setting over the fading green of the trees, bushes, and grass along the road where I was walking. It was my birthday, and I had decided to spend it alone in the hopes that I might receive a special experience from God. While looking at the beautiful sunset and wondering if I would be given such a gift, I was suddenly filled with the heart of God. A melting love flooded me. I felt the eternal and the infinite heart of God while standing in the world of space and time. I felt as if I was in heaven, although I was simply walking down an old abandoned asphalt road in a quiet Texas park. Another intense experience of this kind happened on a bright starry night when I was walking along the shore of Benbrook Lake with my dog, Monty, running in front of me. I looked up at the bright night sky and saw with astonishment that the stars seem to be circling above my head. I literally shook my head to clear what I thought was some misperception, but the stars continued to circle. I wasn't dizzy. I certainly wasn't high and, in fact, I wasn't even frightened. I stood there, head back, mouth gaping, arms dangling—not questioning the physics of what was going on or my sanity, but just receiving—as a stream of white light pulsing with stars drove down into my mind. Instinctively I sank down onto the ground and closed my eyes to fully take in the experience. As I looked inward with my mind's eye, I could still see and feel the starry light pouring into my brain and forming a healing, loving circle of light that moved around and around my head and then flowed into my body. I sat there for what must have been an hour, wrapped in ecstasy.

When we have reconnected with the Divine within us and have received the heart of God, we no longer feel separation or alienation; rather, we feel as if we are home again. We feel as though the journey is over and we have reached our destination. It is here that we find self-esteem or a sense of worthiness, our true specialness, and receive our inner love. We no longer need the false specialness or external love acquired through our holding relationships with people, things, and actions in the world around us. The feeling of being one with nature and the universe experienced in earlier stages of a mystical encounter is transformed into what Martin Buber calls the I-Thou relationship. We have surfed the breath of life and united with the "Eye of the Great Spirit."

Most of the time when we become filled with such Divine love, it spills over not only in tears of joy but also in a deep sense of gratitude for life and our existence in it. Our connection with the Divine also results in the receipt of the other fruits of our Divine nature. We are also filled with the fruits of the spirit, which Galatians 5:22-23 tells us are "love, joy, peace, long-suffering, gentleness, goodness, faith, meekness, temperance..." One of my earliest experiences of other fruits of the Spirit occurred while lying on a waterbed in a small house that I rented during my graduate school years. It was around Easter and I was just lying there looking at the overhead light fixture when suddenly, like a transforming cloud in the sky, it took on what appeared to be the face of God. Upon seeing this face, I was immediately filled with joy. For days,

I walked around filled with joy—it was like experiencing the infinite childlike joy of God.

A Canadian psychiatrist, R.M. Bucke, coined the term "Cosmic Consciousness" to describe what I am calling the Receiving Stage of the mystical experience. According to Dr. Bucke, the prime characteristic of Cosmic Consciousness is a consciousness of the cosmos, that is, of the life and order of the universe. Along with the consciousness of the cosmos there occurs an intellectual and light moment which alone would place the individual on a new plane in existence —would make him almost a member of the new species. To this is added a state of moral exultation, and an indescribable feeling of elevation, elation, and joyousness, and a quickening of the moral sense, which is fully as striking and more important than is the enhanced intellectual power. With these come what may be called a sense of immortality, a consciousness of eternal life, not a conviction that he shall have this, but the consciousness and that he has it already.

Dr. Bucke maintains that cosmic consciousness is a new stage in the evolution of man. Gary Zukav and Linda Francis in *The Mind of the Soul* also believe that we are evolving from what they call five-sensory humans to multisensory humans. They maintain that multisensory humans seek authentic power by aligning themselves with the soul. I am personally inclined more to the ideas of traditional Christianity and *A Course in Miracles*—that man was created in the image of God. I Thessalonians 5:5 reminds us, "Ye are all children of light, and children of the day: we are not of the night, nor of darkness." Thus, experiences of the Divine reflect a return to our basic nature—a reclaiming of the image of God within us rather than some new stage in the evolution of man.

Jesus' behavior and His teachings suggest to me that he lived in the Receiving stage. Although William James suggested that we typically remain in a mystical state at most an hour or two, Jesus appears to have been an exception. His teachings focus on acquiring many characteristics of the Receiving stage and he gave us the Law of Forgiveness to accomplish the task.

The final stage of a Divine encounter is what I call the Extending Stage because it involves extending the heart of God that we received in the preceding stage back into the everyday world in which we live. In *A Return to Love*, Marianne Williamson maintains that "we came here to co-create with God by extending love." Only when we "expand our compassion," she writes in *Healing the Soul of America*, can we undo "oppression and injustice." She stresses that we need to "blend love and politics." Love by its very nature desires to extend itself and unite with others. Therefore, when we are filled with Divine love, we yearn to extend it back into the world. Moreover, it is through extending what we have received that we learn of our inner power. As a result, we no longer need to look for power outside of ourselves in holding relationships with the world. Our relationships with other people show greater sensitivity, tolerance, and compassion than before we receive this love. We experience real personality integration, as well as a sense of personal worth coupled with the letting go of our ego defense.

Both Buddhism and Christianity speak of extending compassion and helping others. The Mahayana and Theravada sects of Buddhism believe the bodhisattva's goal is to lead humankind to enlightenment. The bodhisattva has achieved enlightenment but chooses to forego Nirvana for a life of helping others reach it and thus become liberated from the cycle of rebirth. The bodhisattva according to both sects can be characterized as compassionate, selfless, wise, and a servant to others. Andrew Harvey in *The Essential Mystics* characterizes Christianity as "the way of love in action." Always being filled with Divine love, it follows that Jesus would yearn to extend this love into the world. We can see such a desire in His teachings throughout the New Testament. Jesus taught that we should be mirrors reflecting the love of God into the world.

> But I say unto you, Love your enemies, bless
> them that curse you, do good to them that hate
> you, and pray for them who despitefully use you,
> and persecute you. Matthew 5:44

> A new commandment I give unto you, That ye
> love one another; as I have loved you, that ye
> also love one another. John 13:34.

Jesus taught that the way to express love in the world is by helping others. Most people can understand intellectually what Jesus is teaching about love and helping others but many lack the experiential basis for understanding this teaching. "The love so many of us would like to see injected into the veins of civilization," writes Marianne Williamson, "must first pour into us." Without a personal experience of divine love, we can become spiritual parrots squawking endless scriptures and performing mindless deeds that only mimic the actions of divine love. We base our words and deeds on only an intellectual understanding of Jesus' teachings. As a result, our words and actions often fail to meet the needs of others. Such actions take the guise discussed in I Corinthians 13:1-3:

> Though I speak with the tongues of men and of
> angels, and have not love, I am become as sounding
> bronze, or a tinkling cymbal.
> And though I have the gift of prophecy, and understand
> all mysteries, and all knowledge; and though I have all
> faith, so that I could remove mountains, and have not
> love, I am nothing.
> And though I bestow all my goods to feed the poor,
> and though I give my body to be burned, and have

When I have been filled with such divine love, I return to everyday life with a renewed desire to help people in my psychological practice. I find that my insights into patients' problems are clearer, and my level of empathy greatly improves as a result of such experiences. With the passage of time, however, I lapse back into my negative emotions and holding relationships. When this happens, I simply return for another experience of the Divine. Huston Smith in *The World's Religions* points out that Buddha withdrew from the world for 6 years, and then returned from his venture into the wilderness to help others. He noted that each year Buddha worked for about nine months then retreated for about three months during the rainy season. He would then return from his venture into the wilderness to help others. And every day, too, he would retreat from the world for a while, turn his attention inward, and reconnect with the Divine within him. Jesus is also reported to have withdrawn into the wilderness for renewal and to commune with God. On the eve of His crucifixion, He is reported to have gone into the Garden of Gethsemane alone to pray.

In summation, a mystical encounter involves six stages that we can experience when we let go of our holding relationships by using some form of the Law of Forgiveness. Each stage is a step toward the Divine and should be considered holy. We should enjoy whatever stage we are in rather than attempt to achieve another stage. The first three stages involve undoing what Eastern religions call the subject-object dichotomy. By letting go of our holding relationships with people, things, and actions that bind us to the world, we become aware of our inner being and its separation from nature. As we again use the principle of forgiveness and let go of our separation from the external world, we join nature and become one with it. In this stage of a Divine encounter, we experience ourselves as separate but keen observers of flowing rivers of sensation. We can sense the heartbeat of the universe in the appearances of the world around us. We can see, feel, touch, and hear this heartbeat in the various manifestations of nature that surround us. We also experience ourselves as being in the here-and-now rather than in the there-and-then. With this first stage of letting go, an awareness of our inner love emerges and creates a desire to join with the world. In the second stage, the Sensory-Synchronizing stage, we experience the harmony and unity of the sensory world as well as an awareness of its infinite nature. Here we become aware that the heartbeat of the universe is ordered and infinite. We still, however, experience ourselves as separate from nature. As in the preceding stage, we see light glistening off the sensory world but the love we feel is greater. And this love urges us onward to the next stage of the mystical encounter, the Kinesthetic-Cognitive stage. Here, we experience ourselves as surfing the sensory world and being at-one with nature. At times, we can lose our self-awareness in identification with nature. We join the heartbeat of the Universe, and at times, in identifying with the Universally beating heart we lose awareness of our individually beating one. We experience the world and ourselves in the here-and-now as before but with the additional sense that everything-is-as-it-should-be.

Love continues to grow in this stage and propels us forward to the remaining three stages of a Divine encounter, which involve letting go of our experience of oneness with nature. This results in a shift of direction inward, and we discover that the unity, order, and infinity are within us, rather than outward in the world of nature. We surf inward within ourselves and experience at-onement with the Divine, and we are bathed in light. When we let go of this experience, we flow through the door into eternity and surf with the "breath of life." We flow at-one with Universal Being or the Zero Energy Field. We join the heartbeat behind the world of appearances and flow with the waves of energy that produce the pulsing rhythms of the sensory world. We feel close to our real home, and love for the Divine permeates us and creates within us a sense of gratitude for our existence. In the Receiving stage, we experience a personal connection with the Divine and receive the heart of God. Love floods us in a type of spiritual orgasm. We have joined with the source of the heartbeat—the heart of God. We have joined with the Love that extends itself across the expanse of our seen and unseen world. Finally, in the Extending Stage, we return to the world to share the fruits that we have received from our encounter with the Divine. Like a pebble dropped into a pool of water, we now extend this heartbeat of love back into the world around us.

It is clear that different religions focus on different aspects of a mystical experience or Divine encounter. For example, Native American religions seem to emphasize the first three stages of such an experience. They point to the order and unity of nature and our need to live in harmony with it. Animals as well as such inanimate objects as the sky, sun, moon and earth are believed to possess sacred powers according to Charles Monroe in *World Religions*, and therefore, are gods and can be worshipped. He notes that Native Americans generally see a single cosmos that serves to nourish them; therefore, they don't need to challenge, control, or escape from it. Salvation from the world is not their ultimate goal. Life after death "tends to be a shadowy existence within this single domain." Monroe also points out that some early forms of Hinduism emphasize worshipping nature, which was believed to be endowed with sacred power. They believe in an impersonal, absolute, and unknowable God, called Brahman, but differ from Native Americans in believing in a pantheon of personal gods that serve as manifestations of Brahman. According to Huston Smith in *The World's Religions,* the famous Navajo artist Carl Gorman said that among Navajos, "The Supreme Being is not named because he is unknowable. He is simply the unknown Power. We worship him through his creation for he is everything in his creation. The various forms of creation have some of his spirit within them." From this we can conclude that Navajos would not believe that we can become one with Universal Being as described in the Being stage of a mystical experience or that we can receive the heart of God in the Receiving stage. Rather they would be more likely to seek some joining and living in harmony with the world around them. In short, they could best identify with the first three stages of an encounter with the Divine.

Eastern religions such as Buddhism, some sects of Hinduism, and Zen Buddhism teach that the world is "Maya" or illusion and that we should try to escape it in favor of joining with Universal Being rather than worshipping it or merely seeking to live in harmony with it. These religions focus on teaching methods to overcome the subject/object dichotomy or pass beyond the first three stages of a Divine encounter to unite with Universal Being or enter the Being stage. Jews, Christians, and Muslims distinguish between the physical and spiritual worlds, but they believe that the physical world is real and created by a personal transcendent God. Like the adherents of many Eastern religions, they believe that we should not become entrapped in the physical world; however, they differ in believing that we should have a committed and loving relationship to a personal God. And some sects of Hinduism, those using bhakti and karma yoga also teach that we can unite with a personal God through love and worship. Thus Judaism, Christianity,

Islam, and some sects of Hinduism can be thought of as focusing more on the Receiving and Extending stages of a Divine encounter. Buddhists do not believe in a personal deity but do emphasize compassion toward other beings. They would not, therefore, seek the heart of God or interpret the love felt in the Receiving stage as coming from an encounter with a personal God. But Buddhism's emphasis on compassion suggests an affinity with the idea of giving love back to the world as in the Extending stage. It's as if Buddhism tries to undo the first three stages in order to join with Universal Being experienced in the Being stage and then jumps to the Extending stage, where the emphasis is on extending love and "Bliss" back into the world to help others.

Unfortunately, the diversity of religious views has provided fertile ground for religious bigotry and prejudice. People in all faiths, like wolves marking their territory, have drawn circles of separation around themselves, excluding others as infidels and hell-bound. In *Pluralism in the World Religions*, Harold Coward discusses a number of propositions that he believes can facilitate dialogue between the different religious. He maintains that religions are alike in believing "that God, Brahman, or dharma is a transcendent reality which is over and above the mundane and which cannot be fully conceptualized." And he sees the religions as different principally in the methods by which they attempt to achieve an experience of transcendent reality. But my own studies and experiences have led me to believe that these seemingly different methods are in fact, alike because they are simply different expressions of the same Law of Forgiveness. They are all attempts to undo our attachments or holding relationships with the world of people, things, and actions that block our connection to the Divine.

Rather than letting superficial differences between religions separate and divide us, why can't we focus on their similarities, which can serve to unite us? On the level of content, all religions are seeking union with the Divine and all use the basic principle of forgiveness to achieve it. To me, the main difference between religions is the experience of the Divine that is reported by its founder and later codified by its disciples. But instead of judging and condemning the experiences of the Divine reported in other religions, wouldn't we gain more by accepting and integrating them? Why can't we view different religions as merely focusing on differing stages of a mystical experience and acknowledge that each child in the universe has a right to learn, experience, and dwell in whatever stage he or she needs for spiritual progress? Wouldn't such an inclusive view lead us to the whole truth and prevent territorial battles of separation and condemnation?

As D. E. Harding said in *Hierarchy of Heaven and Earth*, we commit errors of omission in our search for the truth. For example, if we ponder the truth of an apple, the person who sees all aspects of the apple has the best grasp of the true nature of the apple. If we focus on only one or two aspects of the apple, say color or shape, to the exclusion of other aspects, our understanding of it is not whole but distorted by what we exclude. In a similar manner, if we consider only one or two stages of the mystical experience as true or valid to the exclusion of others, we will commit errors of omission and distort our spiritual reality. If we elevate or eliminate stages of the experience to the exclusion of others, we are forming holding relationships with them that can block our spiritual progress. Such behavior would also prevent the discovery of more stages and new revelations of the Divine.

In my search for truth, I have found that many religions have cast their light on my path. Native American beliefs taught me the importance of loving and living at-one with nature. The music of Native American artists such as Douglas Spotted Eagle, Joanne Shenandoah, David and Steve Gordon and Sharon Burch, as well as the groups producing collections of chants such as "Sacred Spirit I and II", "Tribal Voices and Legends", and "Between Father Sky and Mother Earth" was of immense help to me in discovering and feeling the first three stages of a Divine encounter. Eastern religious views helped me to understand how my mind contributes to the subject-object dichotomy and how to undo that effect with one-pointed concentration, thereby enabling me to join with the state of Being that lies behind the universe. Finally, my Judeo-Christian roots, which emphasize cultivating a personal, loving relationship with the Divine, helped me realize that beyond the Being stage lies the heart of God in the Receiving stage. These spiritual roots emphasized extending love back into the world. Most importantly, my Christian roots introduced the Law of forgiveness, the main principle behind all healing and the basic activity to reconnect with the Divine or zero-energy field.

# References

Adams, J. Donald. *Poems of Ralph Waldo Emerson*. New York, NY: Thomas Y. Crowell Company, 1965.

Alighieri, Dante. *The Divine Comedy*. Translated by C.H. Sisson Oxford, NY, Oxford University Press, 1993.

Amir Hamzah 'One Alone' trans. By A.H. Johns in *Malayan & Indonesian Studies*, Ed. John Bastin and R. Roolvik. London, England: Oxford University Press, 1964 pp 318-319.

Barrett, William. *Zen Buddhism: Selected Writings of D.T. Suzuki*. Garden City, NY: Doubleday Anchor Books, 1956.

Beard, Gregg. *The Divine Matrix*. Carlsbad, CA: Hay House, 2007.

Bearden, Gregg. *Resilience from the Heart: The Power to Thrive in Life's Extremes.* Carlsbad, CA: Hay House, 2014

Bhaktivedanta, Swami A.C. *The Bhagavad Gita As It Is*. New York, NY: Collier Books, 1968.

Black Elk. *Black Elk Speaks.* Transcribed by John G. Niehardt. Lincoln, NE: University of Nebraska Press, 1961.

Blavatsky, Helen Petrovna. *Isis Unveiled.* Digital Edition 2013.

Browning, Robert. "Pippa Passes" from Sprague, R. *Poems of Robert Browning*. New York, NY: Thomas Y. Cromwell Company, 1964.

Buah, Samuel A. *Ye are Gods: The Extraordinary Life of the Sons of God.* 2016

Bucke, R.M. *Cosmic Consciousness*. New York, NY: E.P. Dutton, 1969.

Cameron, Linda N., Ph.D. *Cosmic Surfing.* Lincoln, NE: iUniverse, Inc, 2004.

Cannon, W.B. *The Wisdom of the Body.* New York, NY: Norton, 1932.

Casarjian, Robin. *Forgiveness: A Bold Choice for a Peaceful Heart.* New York, NY: Bantam Books, 1992.

Childre, D.L. *Cut-Thru.* Boulder Creek, CA: Planetary Publications, 1996.

Childre, D.L., Martin, Howard, & Beech, Donna. *The HeartMath Solution*. New York, NY: Harper One Publishing, 1999.

Cleary, Thomas. *The Essential Koran: The Heart of Islam.* New York, NY: Harper & Collins Publishers, 1993.

Coward, Harold. *Pluralism in the World Religions*. Oxford, England: One World Publications, 2000.

de Chardin, Pierre Teilhard. *The Phenomenon of Man* in *The Great Library Collection* by R.P. Pryne 2015.

Eckhart, Meister. *Sermons and Treatises, 2 Volumes*. Translated and edited by M. O'C Walshe Element Books, 1979-1987.

Ellmann, R. *The New Oxford Book of American Verse*. New York, MY: Oxford University Press, 1976.

Emerson, Ralph Waldo. "Circles" In *Ralph Waldo Emerson: Essays and Poems*. New York, NY. The Library of America College Edition, 1996.

Evans-Wentz, W.Y. *The Tibetan Book of the Dead*. London, England: Oxford University Press, 1960.

Fillmore, Charles. *The Twelve Powers of Man*. Unity Village, MO: Unity School of Christianity 1995.

Finley, Guy. **The** *Secret of Letting Go*. St. Paul, MN: Llewellyn Publications, 2002.

Ford, Debbie. **The** *Dark Side of the Light Chasers*. New York, NY: Riverhead Books, 1998.

Gilbert, R.A. *The Elements of Mysticism*. Boston, MA: Element Books, 1998.

Griffiths, Bebe. *Return to the Center*. Springfield, IL: Templegate, 1977.

Goldman, Jonathan. *The Divine Name*: *The Sound That Can Change the World*. Carlsbad, California: Hay House, 2010.

Harding, D.E. *The Hierarchy of Heaven and Earth*. New York, NY, Harper, 1953.

Hardy, Sir Alister. **The** *Spiritual Nature of Man: A Study of contemporary Religious Experience*. OUP, 1979.

Harvey, Andrew. *The Way of Passion: A Celebration of Rumi*. Berkley, CA: Frog, LTD, 1994 Translator of Rumi's poem "Every particle of the World is a Mirror."

James, William. *Varieties of Religious Experience*. New York, NY: The New American library of World Literature, 1958.

Jampolsky, G.C. *Forgiveness: The Greatest Healer of All*. Hillsboro, OR: Beyond Words Publishing, Inc., 1999.

Jones, Frank Pierce. *Body Awareness in Action: A Study of the Alexander Technique*.

New York, NY: Schocken Books, 1976.

Jung, C. G. *Memories, Dreams, Reflections*. New York, NY: Random Books, 1961, p. 94.

Jung, C.G. *The Symbolic Life, Collective Works of Carl Jung, Volume 18*. Princeton, NJ: University Press, 1973 p. 577.

Laski, Marghanita Ecstasy: *A Study of Some Secular & Religious Experiences*. Cresset Press, 1961.

Lawrence, Bro and Laubach, Frank. *Practicing His Presence*. Syracuse. NY: New Readers Press, 1973.

Luskin, Fred. *Forgive for Good*. New York, NY: Harper Collins, 2000.

Luk, A. D. K. **Law of Life, Book 1.** Oklahoma City, OK: A. D. K. Luk Publications, 1972.

Luk, A. D. K. *Law of Life, Book 2.* Oklahoma City, OK: A. D. K. Luk Publications, 1958.

Luk, A. D. K. *Life and Teaching of Jesus and Mary.* Oklahoma City, OK: A. D. K. Luk Publications, 1966.

Luthe, W. (Ed.) *Autogenic Therapy. (Vols. 1-6)* New York, NY: Grune & Stratton,1969.

MacDonald, D. B. *The Religious Attitude and Life of Islam*. New York, NY Hyperion Books, 1985.

Mahmud, Shabestarie. The Rosegarden of Mystery as quoted in Andrew Harvey *The Essential Mystic*, Edison, NJ: Castle Books, 1998.

Martal, Jacques. *The 5 Steps to Achieve Healing*. Quebec, Canada: National Library of Canada, 2014.

May, Robert. *Cosmic Consciousness Revisited*. Rockport, MD: Element Inc, 1993.

McColman, Carl. *The Aspiring Mystic*. Adams Media Corporation, Holbrook, MA, 2000.

McArthur, David & McArthur, Bruce. *The Intelligent Heart.* Virginia Beach, Virginia: Association for Research and Enlightenment, 1997.

Millon, Theodore. *Modern Psychopathology: A Biosocial Approach to Maladaptive Learning and Functioning*. Philadelphia, PA: W.B. Saunders Company, 1969.

Mitchell, Stephen. *The Gospel According to Jesus*. New York, NY: Harper Collins, 1919.

Monroe, Charles. *World Religions*. Amherst, NY: Prometheus Books, 1995.

Moody, Raymond. *Life After Life*. Atlanta, GA: Mockingbird Books, 1975.

Newburn, Kent. *The Wisdom of the Native Americans* Novato, CA New World Library, 1999.

Pagels, Elaine. *The Gnostic Gospels.* New York, NY: Vintage Books, 1981.

Pagels, Heinz. *The Cosmic Code: Quantum Physics as the Language of Nature*. Mineola, NY Dover Publications, 2011.

Paddison, Sara *The Hidden Power of the Heart.* Boulder Creek CA: Planetary Publications, 1992

Prather, Hugh. *The Little Book of Letting. Go* New York, NY: Barnes & Noble, 2000.

Project Gutenberg eBook of the King James Bible, *The King James Bible*, 1989.

Rice, E. *The Five Great Religions*. New York, NY: Four Winds Press, 1973.

Robinson, James M. editor "The Gospel of Saint Thomas" from *The Nag Hammadi Library* San Francisco, CA: Harper & Row Publishers, 1981 pp 123.

Robinson, James M. editor "The Book of Mary" from *The Nag Hammadi Library* San Francisco, CA: Harper & Row Publishers, 1981 pp 123.Rumi, Jalal ud-din Mathnawi-I Manawi Ed. & Trans. in 8 volumes by R.A. Nicholson, Gibb Memorial Trust, 1925-40.

Sandner, Donald. *Navajo Symbols of Healing*. New York, NY: Harcourt Brace Jovanovich, 1979.

Schucman, Helen. *A Course in Miracles*. Tiburon, CA: Foundation for Inner Peace, 1975.

Selye, Hans. *The Stress of Life*. New York, NY: McGraw-Hill, 1976.

Shapiro, F. (1995). *Eye Movement Desensitization and Reprocessing: Basic Principles, Protocols, and Procedures*. New York: Guilford Press, 1995. Shapiro, F. (1995). Eye Movement Desensitization and Reprocessing: Basic Principles, Protocols, and Procedures. New York: Guilford Press.

Smith, Houston. *The World's Religions*. San Francisco, CA: Harper Collins, 1991.

St. Augustine. *The Confessions of Saint Augustine*. Translated by Maria Boulding, O.S.B. Hyde Park, NY New city Press, 1997.

St. John of the Cross. *The Complete Works of Saint John of the Cross*. Westminster, England: Newman Press, 1953.

Stephenson, Jason. *Quantum Physics For beginners: Quantum Mechanics and Quantum Theory Explained*. First Published, 2015.

Stewart, John James. *Story Keepers A Journey into Native American Spirituality*. Nashville, TN: Premium Press America, 2016.

Whitman, Walt. "Song of Myself" In Robert J. Begiebing and Owen Grumbling Medford, NJ, 1990.

Thondup, Tulku. *Enlightened Journey: Buddhist Practice as Daily Life*. Boston, MA: Shambhala Publications Inc, 1995.

Tipping, Colin. *Radical Forgiveness: Making Room for the Miracle*. Marietta, GA: Global 13 Publications, Inc., 2002.

Tolle, Eckhart. *The Power of Now*. Novato, CA: New World Library, 1999.

Walsch, Neale Donald. *Conversations with God*. New York, NY: Berkley Books, 1995.

Walsch, Neale Donald. *Communion with God*. New York, NY: Berkley Books, 2002.

Wapnick, Kenneth. *Forgiveness and Jesus*. Roscoe, NY: Foundation for A Course in Miracles, 1983.

Wiener, Norbert. *The Human Use of Human Beings*. Boston, MA: Houghton Mifflin, 1954.

Williams, Peter. *American Religions: From Their Origins to the Twenty-First Century*. Chicago. IL, 2002.

Williamson, Marianne. *A Return to Love*. New York, NY: Harper Collins Publishers, 1992.

Williamson, Marianne. *Healing the Soul of America*. New York, NY: Touchstone 2000.

Winter, David. *Closer Than a Brother*. Wheaton, IL: Harold Shaw Publishers, 1971.

Wordsworth, William. 'Ode on Intimations of immortality' In Roy J. Cook *One Hundred and One Famous Poems*. Chicago, IL: Contemporary Books, 1958.

Yogananda, Paramahansa. *Autobiography of a Yogi*. Los Angeles, CA: Self-Realization Fellowship Publishers, 1971.

Zodhiates, Spiros, Th. D. and Baker, Warren, D.R.E. (Editors) *Hebrew-Greek Keyword Study Bible KJV*. AMG International, Inc. 2008.

Zukav, Gary & Francis, Linda. *The Heart of the Soul*. New York, NY: Simon & Schuster, 2001.

Zukav, Gary & Francis, Linda. *The Mind of the Soul*. New York, NY: Free Press 2003.

Zukav, Gary. *The Seat of the Soul*. New York, NY: Fireside Book, 1990.

Wommack, Andrew. *Discover the Keys to Staying Full of God*. Tulsa, OK: Harrison House Publishers, 2008.

Printed in the United States
by Baker & Taylor Publisher Services

Printed in the United States
by Baker & Taylor Publisher Services